THE wild JOURNEY

MY CROSSROADS OF OVERCOMING FEAR, DEPRESSION & ANXIETY

DREW GLEBOW

By John Lennon

First published by Ultimate World Publishing 2023
Copyright © 2023 Drew Glebow

ISBN

Paperback: 978-1-922982-58-2
Ebook: 978-1-922982-59-9

Drew Glebow has asserted his rights under the Copyright, Designs and Patents Act 1988 to be identified as the author of this work. The information in this book is based on the author's experiences and opinions. The publisher specifically disclaims responsibility for any adverse consequences which may result from use of the information contained herein. Permission to use information has been sought by the author. Any breaches will be rectified in further editions of the book.

All rights reserved. No part of this publication may be reproduced, stored in or introduced into a retrieval system, or transmitted in any form, or by any means (electronic, mechanical, photocopying, recording or otherwise) without the prior written permission of the author. Any person who does any unauthorised act in relation to this publication may be liable to criminal prosecution and civil claims for damages. Enquiries should be made through the publisher.

Cover design: Ultimate World Publishing
Layout and typesetting: Ultimate World Publishing
Editor: James Salmon

Ultimate World Publishing
Diamond Creek,
Victoria Australia 3089
www.writeabook.com.au

DEDICATION

I dedicate this book to my late father, Gregory George Glebow. He was born on 17 April 1949 and passed away on 15 January 2021. I love my dad and I will always remember his great intentions and the lovely moments he offered in life. The way he dealt with things was not his fault due to the childhood trauma he was exposed to. He passed away with family around him. He will be missed.

I also dedicate this book to my mum Lyn Anderson who has been there through all the good times and bad times throughout my life. I was always fed great meals, loved, and cared for. My mum has also taught me many things to be aware of in life and is still there for me today.

And this book will form an ongoing legacy once I've moved on from this planet to my two beautiful daughters Charlie Glebow and Kelsey Glebow, who have inspired me so much through the course of their existence, to be motivated and to be a better version of myself. You girls are my everything and will always be my babies.

I also make mention of everyone that's traveled my path, either past, present, or in the future, who has assisted me and been a positive light in my life. I thank you and dedicate this book to those who have not yet begun to explore their journey and discover their true path and their right to be the better, best version of themselves.

The following information in this book is to the very best of my recollection of experiences.

Dedication

CONTENTS

Dedication	v
Chapter 1: The Longest Dark	1
Chapter 2: The Soldier Within	7
Chapter 3: Deployment	15
Chapter 4: Civil Life	23
Chapter 5: Toxic	29
Chapter 6: Marriage	39
Chapter 7: Pin Up Boy	49
Chapter 8: Diagnosis	57
Chapter 9: Crossroads	65
Chapter 10: Redefining Moments	75
Chapter 11: Fear, Anxiety & Depression	83
Chapter 12: Healed	91
About The Author	97
Offerings	99
Acknowledgment	100

Chapter 1

THE LONGEST DARK

Abandoned, accused, alone, angry, anxious, ashamed, attacked, bitter, depressed, deprived. Failure, insulted, left out, lonely, lost. Stupid, shattered, unprotected, and vulnerable. These were just a few of the thoughts and feelings running through my head on this particular day. This day was the longest day of darkness I've ever encountered in my life.

This day was the crunch day. This day, without me realising it at that point in time, was going to be the day that was absolutely going to change my life forever. But at that point, I had no idea. I didn't know what to do. This day was just like any other day in my life, rinse and repeat, rinse and repeat. This was my life; it was truly like the movie Groundhog Day.

At this point in time, I was working for a city council, in a team of six under the instructions of a coordinator within this team. We were the animal attack team within the organisation of local government enforcement. Our job was to go out and obviously deal with dog attack complaints, investigate, and reach an outcome. In comparison to the police service, we were equivalent to detectives – we were regarded as senior investigative officers. We were an investigative team who would go out and investigate any dog attack that constituted fear and alarm or an actual bite or an attack in the physical sense. So anywhere from fear right through to alarm.

We had a team that would go out to the initial situation, as it was called, secure the scene, and then obtain preliminary statements, photographs, and anything that could be obtained. They would then pass those complaints on to us, and our job was to cover all of the city. We were split up into different areas of the city, and not all six of us were on all the time except for Thursdays. But most of the time we were running about two or four people that would have to cover these areas and ongoing investigations.

Unfortunately, what was happening in this workplace was segregation, discrimination, favoritism, and simple workplace bullying. There were all sorts of things running through the system, not just in our area, but right throughout local government. It was right within the state government and within the Commonwealth government, because guess what, I worked in all three of those areas as well. We'll get to that later. As I worked for the local government, I found it was incestual in the sense everyone knew someone who was a family member. As we all got recruited you knew it was just a matter of time before that knife got twisted in your back and you would be put on your ass. We all eventually got that welcome handshake with that knife jabbed in our back.

Unfortunately, on this day it was my time, and the knife was twisted deep. I had been fighting the fight with my coordinator for some time now. I'd had a mate whom I was fighting back-to-back with. We'd been looking out for each other up till now, but now I didn't have that, I didn't have that safety. I didn't have the security of another good person. So, what happened from here was just the result of an ongoing battle that I had with the ethics that were in that particular area of the workplace.

To give you an example, I mean, our coordinator didn't just do the job. He took the job outside of the job. On his days off, he'd be ringing people within that team and talking to them and trying to find out what other team members were doing or weren't doing. There was a friendship and bond outside the workplace. There were four up against me.

On this day I sat there at my desk feeling like I had such a massive weight over me. I came in early that morning like I normally would, starting at 6 am and finishing at 2 pm. I was confronted by my coordinator at some point – he sat there opposite me two seats away so he could watch what I do. Behind me was his friend who would listen to and watch what I did. So, I was always under micromanagement. Always being scrutinised for everything I did. I fought and fought and fought but on this particular day, the bastard just wasn't in me anymore. I just couldn't do it anymore. I was having a meltdown. I was defeated. I just went, I'm out, I'm done.

When I sat at my computer there were from memory 30 odd jobs. And that was very high, very very high – especially when you had KPIs and someone riding you, deliberately setting you up for failure. Each and every day gave me a workload that couldn't be written off in a timely manner. They were pushing me out because I didn't fall within the fold, and this was their way of doing it. I didn't lower my ethics; I didn't lower my moral standards to be pushed into this cult of odd behavior. I had colleagues who got excited about putting people's pets down and having a picture board of their dog's faces with their eyes etched out as they were destroyed, to name just one odd behavioral habit.

So, I sat there, and I remember my legs just felt like jelly and those negative words screamed through every part of my body, my brain, my spirit, my soul, sitting there I just felt like I had ten people sitting on top of me. I felt like I couldn't breathe. And I just sat there looking at that screen going, I can't do this anymore. I just recently had given up a 14-year marriage and all I could think of was my two daughters. This was also being used against me as well, everything and anything that could be used against me was being used against me to get me out of that team because I didn't fall into what they wanted. That's why my mate left and joined the police service – he had enough of the poor behavior too. So, I sat there, and I just said what do I do?

I grabbed my bag, which was a little green bag that was given to us by the council as part of our work equipment. I went through the little filing cabinet that was sitting next to me at the desk there. Basically, all I had was a desk in front of me, a laptop setup, a keyboard, a mouse, and a few other bits and bobs, and then beside me, I had like a little lockable filing cabinet. A little thing on wheels that carried all my personal effects folders; anything that was confidential or worth value was inside of that. I opened it up and just started grabbing stuff that was relevant to me that I thought that I'd need because, at this point, my intention was to never come back. I just wanted, and I needed, to leave. I couldn't come back.

The Longest Dark

So, while at my desk I looked at the coordinator, and everything he was doing was running through my brain. What he was trying to do, how he was doing it, where this was going to go, and how it was going to end up. And you know, throughout that whole day I couldn't eat. I had a couple of sips of water, but my body was in flight mode. I basically remember sitting there just looking at those jobs. I didn't do any work that day, not one because I didn't know what to do. I didn't know so it came to a point where it was getting close to 2 pm. I was on the run home now, I thought you know what, I can do this, I can stick this out till two. I've gone this far today. And you know the funny thing about the whole day is that nobody came near me. Nobody said anything to me, and I didn't even get one phone call from a customer, nothing. It was almost like I was sitting in another parallel universe with the same outlook, same features, and same settings, but just there was no connection to anyone. It was like I was invisible, this energy or this field around me where people could sense not to go near me or fuck with me today. But by the same token, no one came over to me and asked if I was all right, and I was far, far from okay.

When two o'clock came, I had my bag packed. I left everything they gave me, including my ID, everything there that I thought they would chase me for. I just took my personal effects. I walked out that door knowing I could not get back in without my ID. I didn't say anything, and I didn't tell anyone to get fucked I just walked out the door, and I went home, and I drank myself silly that night. At that point, I had a partner, and I remember just bouncing off the partner, who said, "You can't keep doing this. You just can't. You can't go back. You can't go back.

So, I said, "Well, the only thing I can do is go on stress leave". It was the only thing I could do. Many of us went on stress leave. Many of us were forced to go on stress leave – this was how the departments in our local government worked. And so, I did it. I rang up the next day and said I'm not well and I'm on stress leave because of workplace bullying. And that was the beginning of my standing up for myself and fighting a new ethical fight. That was the beginning of what was then going to be a formal investigation into that team and the conduct, and in the end, uncovering the misbehaving and the inappropriate things that that team was doing. And thankfully, I teamed up with my mate and he also helped me with the investigation. He was a supporting witness and we got statements from him as well. And we fought them, and we fought them all.

And you know, I never went back again. I never went back and put my foot in that workplace again, other than in town in the city where I had to go to a formal interview to see if they could relocate me. I just basically told him that there was no place he could relocate me that could be far enough to stop me from hurting any of those people for what they've done to me. And from there they gave me a payout and sent me on my way and I've never, ever to this day looked back and regretted the move that I took that day, even though it was the hardest thing I've ever done and the darkest day of my life. It was also the best day of my life when I look back because I did the right thing. I moved forward and I'm still moving forward in life, and I've succeeded in doing that by doing and getting rid of toxic, negative, egotistical, narcissistic people and environments from my life.

Chapter 2

THE SOLDIER WITHIN

Back before 1991, ever since I was a child, I'd always wanted to become one of two things. The first of those two things was a police officer. The second was a soldier, an army man. And back when I was going through school, I never really liked it too much; it was never my forte. I went through and left school with the agreement with my mother that I got a full-time job. This was back at the beginning of year 10.

I've always been a person that liked money. I always like to have my own money and buy my own things; I was always self-sufficient. I found it rewarding to always earn my money and be able to hold it and do what I want with it.

After I left school, I ended up going and working in retail. I worked at Big W, working in mainly the men's clothing department. And I enjoyed it. Of course, at that point in time,

The Wild Journey

you know, I was only 16 moving into being 17. When I went through and worked there, I made friendships and obviously found my feet in the work career lifestyle. When I got enough experience there, I got bored and wanted to join the police force, but unfortunately for me, I was knocked back and told that I passed everything except the aptitude tests. That I didn't meet the requirements of their educational level and what they wanted was a minimum of 200 hours of diplomacy to move forward with the selection process. I did end up starting TAFE but being a kid and studying… The kid in me wanted to play. And you know, my mum was always there for me and helped me with whatever my choices were.

My wanting to be a soldier was still burning with desire and so I thought I would try this path. So, my mother and I went into Brisbane city one day to the Defence Recruiting Office and sat down with a person who was obviously a recruiting officer, and they gave me a package and spoke to me and told me about this lifestyle, this career. That day I took my package, and I went away, and I just kept looking at it and I kept looking at the pictures and just kept seeing myself there you know, and I wanted this so bad. So, I started the recruitment process.

Again I was challenged by this move, I always seem to be challenged by something that tries to prohibit me and stop me from doing something I desire. This time it was my hearing. So, I went from specialist to specialist till the defence force accepted that what I had was not going to affect my service with them. So, what I was about to do was a massive yet serious contract with the government. I was handing my mind, my body, and my spirit over to the defence force, who was going to become my new family.

Having said all this, there was still one round of the selection process left: the psychiatric test. And I remember a few people telling me, whatever you do, don't go in there and tell them you want to kill people, or you want a gun, whatever they say. I remember that day the psych said, "Are you prepared to die for your country?" My answer was, "Yes I am". He leaned forward and said, "That's the wrong answer". By now I just kept thinking I'd screwed this up. He continued to say, "Let them die for theirs". He then shook my hand and said well done.

So the day came when I was leaving home at the age of 17 to become a soldier in my newly chosen career. I remember as I was heading to the door my dad was there and like with any proud dad giving me a handshake or hug caused an altercation and in turn caused me to punch him in the mouth. I'll never forget that moment. Why? Because while I was training over the course of the next few weeks I had to deal with an open cut from his tooth in my knuckle and it was highly infected due to his dirty mouth. This really impacted my training. So out the door with my mum, I went, and that was my parting gift from my dad.

I parted ways from Mum on a bus from Brisbane where I signed my life away for four years of service. And as I headed to Kapooka I was scared, nervous, and excited all rolled into one. A boy on a bus with strangers. Oddly it was like going off to jail, not that I have been there. We then jumped onto a plane and then a bus where I was confronted with beefy men, soldiers in uniform. No smiles, no welcome, no nothing. Just told to get our belongings and get on the bus. We boarded the bus then we arrived later at the Kapooka Training Centre, which would be my home for the next 13 weeks.

The Wild Journey

After a few days of settling in we were called to the hallway. At that moment everything changed.

I stood there with over 40 people that I'd met. I had no real bonded relationships or friendships with anyone like that. The sergeant and corporals came out and were screaming and yelling aggressively at us all. I was yelled at about an inch away from my face, I was told that my mother was a slut along with many other disgusting things. I was told that I was a fuckup and that I would never again walk in the gutter, only civilians walk in gutters. We were no longer civilians; we were now soldiers. We were above being civilians. From there it was just total abuse, there was just total disrespect, and I was treated along with everyone else, like absolute shit.

The idea whilst we were at Kapooka was to break us down from civilians and rebuild us into men, into soldiers. And trust me, they did that in 13 weeks. But it didn't stop there, because I then had to transfer and then go over to Singleton where I would get more defined training in the role of an infantry soldier. See, at this point in time, I wanted to be in the Army because the Gulf War had started in 1991. I was watching it on television every day. And I just kept saying to myself, I want in, I want to go over there, and I want to fight. I wanted a part of the action, I wanted to be part of that action.

They told everyone that there was a high chance that they would end up going over to the Gulf War. All right, so we had this in the back of our minds, right? And it was quite funny as I heard the corporal say what do you want to do? What trade, what special areas do you want to do? And most of us said infantry, but you'd hear some say payroll, transport, engineer, and so on. The corporal then said, "Excellent, because all of you are going into the infantry". Poor bastards.

After beginning with over 40 people, we marched out from memory with 11 of us. We'd had people go AWOL. We had people get bashed. Yeah, people were bashed by corporals. There were investigations going on. Probably nothing ever came out of it. Who knows? I never heard anything. There were people that were obviously getting seriously injured, unreasonably seriously injured. Because we were pushed beyond the limits and beyond expectations. So, we had people dropping like flies left, right, and center.

I was pretty good and would stay under the radar as I was a great shooter and physically fit. All those years of shooting with my dad paid off. I certainly wasn't a heat seeker, which meant that I wasn't a person that obviously drew attention by creating problems. And they used to always pick a heat seeker, and they'd get rid of them, and then they'd pick another to get rid of. That's how they used to be left with the best. I'd hear screams at night, I'd hear recruits being punched at night from my bed. In my mind, it was just like being in prison. I've never been in prison, but to me, it was pretty strict and senseless, and you just had to watch your back in there. It was a different way of life. Because this just wasn't it wasn't a job. This was my way of life.

From there, we ended up marching out, doing all of our training. Then we went from there to Singleton Infantry Training Centre. All we did was friggin dig holes and march. We didn't sleep, we dug holes, and we just went for pack marches all the time. It was insane. Incredibly insane. I look back now, and I just want to know how the hell I did that. I was physically and verbally abused. When I was at Singleton, I was punched twice, by the same corporal. I was punched in the face, and I was punched in the chest. I was shaken and I was spoken to really poorly.

Here I am, a boy, a teenager, coming from a domestic violence situation where my dad used to run me down and want to fight with me, to a new family where my supposed role model was doing the same thing. I couldn't get away from it.

But I survived Singleton. And then I ended up getting deployed in permanent residency up in Townsville, North Queensland, Australia in 1 RAR. I was in Charlie Company 7 platoon. I was a part of Three Section, which was pretty cool and that's where my home was. We had some drop kicks in there, but you get that in any job. I was considered Jube, green, because I was fresh, I was new, and there had been guys up there for years and years and years. I'd only been up there for a short while before being deployed to Somalia as a fighting force, active service deployment. I had only recently turned 18 years of age at this moment.

So, it was back in 1992, when I was on Christmas leave back in Brisbane, that we got warned that we might get called back because we were going to get deployed to Somalia as a fighting force in early 1993. A fighting force wasn't under the UN banner. We didn't wear blue berets, and we weren't peacekeepers because we were a fighting force of 900 soldiers, going in and disarming bandits which are now known as terrorists. The goal was to bring and restore hope to the people of Africa. This was known as Operation Restore Hope. Following orders so that we could provide food, shelter, and safety to the residents of that country.

Before we got there, I remember having a phone conversation with my mum telling her that we were being warned about this possibility. I was coming home on Christmas leave, but we'd been warned that we may get called back to go over to Somalia. She said, "Do you know it's ironic because when I grew up as a young girl and before I had kids, I swore that I would never ever allow the government to send my children, my boys, overseas and transcript them into the military and send them over to fight and die". She told me that she fought against that, but that it was ironic that now I was turning 19 and heading overseas. Generally speaking, that is how I turned from a boy into a man pretty much overnight. The wild journey had begun.

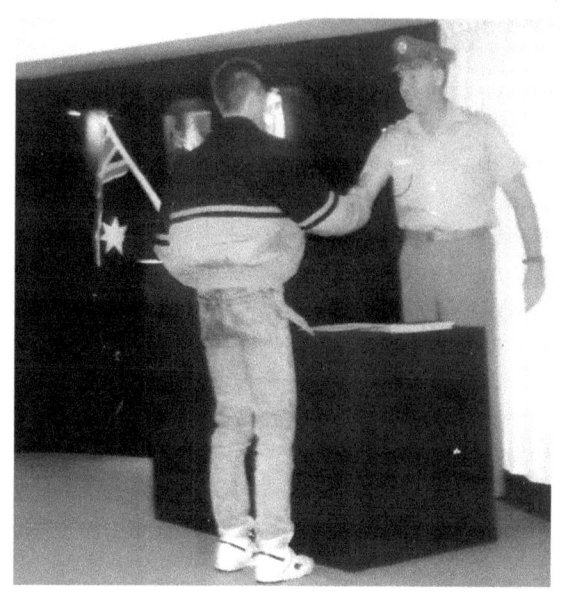

chapter 3

DEPLOYMENT

In December 1992, I was on Christmas leave, when I was sent a telegram advising me that I'd been scripted to come back to Townsville, back to the barracks, as we were being deployed for military active service to Somalia, the Horn of Africa. This would take place for us in around March 1993. We had to get back and train for those supporting roles and understand exactly what we were doing. But basically, for us, we were in support of the United Nations operations with Somalia. We would later find out we would be flown in by civil airline Qantas to a war zone. This was an actual airline passenger jet that people used to obviously travel around and go on holidays in, there was no Hercules or military transport for us on this trip.

I remember at that moment, we also had to learn about the cultures, we had to learn about the do's and don'ts, the languages, the bandits, and everything that you would get in pre-ops. We were going to be a contingent of a 900-person fighting force. So as an infantry battalion, the first battalion, we were the first to go anywhere. And that's exactly what we were doing. Our battalion was going to be the first fighting force to be deployed since Vietnam, in 1962. And we were going over to actually disarm and obviously bring back law and order to a country that had lost it through bandits, which we now refer to as terrorists. Our role was to go in hot and seek out these bandits and provide security and order for food drops and live aid such as medical assistance etc.

Obviously, we had engagement rules and stuff like that. I still remember a few of the boys hanging their heads out the windows in the barracks and yelling out, "We are going to war woohoo, yeah, we're going". We all got excited; one or two of the soldiers might have been a bit nervous or scared, but I can tell you honestly, the majority of us were ready to go. Some of those boys had been up there for years training hard and waiting for this moment. And I was fortunate that I'd rolled in not long beforehand, and I got the opportunity of a lifetime to go, and as I said this hadn't happened since Vietnam 1962.

HOLY SHIT!! This was real. This wasn't training. I remember getting closer to the land of Africa as we were coming to Mogadishu. I remember just looking out the little plane window, and as far as the eye could see was just military equipment and war-torn buildings with chunks taken out of them from weapon fire. I remember getting off that plane as you would going on a holiday in my cams and slouch hat with my little black carry-on bag just being so excited and yet so alive. My eyes were like a possum in the headlights. It was not long after my boots touched the dirt that there was an exchange of gunfire and we had to seek cover. You couldn't distinguish exactly from wherever it came

Deployment

from, but we were being shot at. That was our welcome party from the enemy, to what would be our new home for some time.

We were then transported out to another area called Baidoa where we would live and work for the duration of our time in Somalia. When we arrived, we made our home, a big green canvas tent and a stretcher as a bed that we had to set up on a dump site. Yes, a dump site, so we had to clear that first. This definitely had a one-star rating review only.

Our roles were rotational as a platoon. We would spend a week patrolling, then another doing searches on hot spots, to being on observation points to resting. There were a lot of roles within these rotations, but these were but a few. I remember one of the first roles we did was to head out in convoy on trucks, and it didn't take long when we heard a shot ring out. I remember looking over and seeing a guy a few down from me with blood dripping off his face. He had been clearly shot. His name was Normie. We stopped. What had happened was that the rifle went off due to the rough surface and bumps and the bullet ricocheted and a bit of metal went up and sliced him. But you could see the intensity when we thought he was shot by an enemy. There were people wanting to kill us.

Over time we found the locals over there were absolutely wonderful people. However, I did find in general the men to be extremely lazy. Most men were on a drug called khat. Chewing this native plant gave a stimulant effect which is similar to the coca plant used for making cocaine. Due to this imbalance, I had seen women acting like and being treated like pack horses and carrying a multitude of things like bags of rice/wheat, and water drums on their heads and shoulders, including kids on their backs, and fronts.

The Wild Journey

I remember several moments over there that will never leave me. On one occasion, I was inside a complex and there was a loud noise outside. We went outside with the other soldiers, and a young girl lay on the ground in a pool of blood. Just a very young girl, maybe six from memory. Her head was opened up and her brain was pulsating. She'd been struck by a car, and she was dying. Unfortunately, that young girl did die at that moment. She was picked up by a man and taken away to be buried. That was life over there. That was nothing to people for what they heard, saw, and felt.

Another moment I remember is being on point for OP1. Observation Point One was the main gate to our camp. We monitored who came in and out to simplify things. This particular night we had heard over the radio that an Australian soldier was just shot, and they were bringing in the APC – Armored Personnel Carrier – with him in it for medical attention. I recall seeing this APC racing in through the main gate with the hatch open looking down and seeing this soldier covered in blood. This was later known to be our first loss of life with one of our boys. It was later found he was cleaning his weapon; the weapon was handed over the barrel first, the trigger was pulled, and a bullet at point blank entered his chest. Unfortunately, he did die. There was a lot of loss of life over there during our stay in conflicts with us or around us. Other soldiers received injuries along the way. This was war.

On another particular night, we were rostered as a ready-response group. We went out to a location and got into a firefight shooting into a bush line of bandits. All you could see at night was the flash of the muzzle on the rifle as the rounds zipped past us. When the firefight stopped, we then went in and did a search for any bodies. But you couldn't see anybody, no one remained

Deployment

but the trails of the blood of the people we shot. Often enough, these characters were so super skinny, that the round which we were using, which was 5.56mm, would just clearly go through the body and exit straight out. It wouldn't be enough to tumble and cause enough injury to kill the person, it would just go straight through them. The smaller bullets were designed to cause injury, not so much death, and disrupt the rest of the people in that firefight. We could then take them with us for intel.

But on this particular night, I remember, there were quite a few bandits lying on the ground. And they were dead. They'd been shot by our guys in a firefight, and they came out second best. And they were killed. And I remember one of the sergeants jumping up and down on top of the body of one of the dead bandits because his adrenaline was so pumped, he was jumping up and down and cursing and swearing. And that happened a lot over there, your adrenaline would just kick in and you'd just do some crazy stuff.

There's another incident where we went to a village and I was chasing on foot for kilometres and kilometres, to the stage that three of us got segregated from our platoon, from our section. We didn't see anyone, we lost the vehicle, everything, and were chasing after this bandit that had held this nurse at gunpoint. When we finally caught up with him, we found him, he was trying to camouflage the blood on him by cutting a goat's throat that lay there dying next to him bleeding out as he had a knife in his hand. We held him at rifle point. We had rifles pointed at him, and we were ready to kill him if he made a move on us and didn't drop that knife. One of the big guys, Fletch, ended up doing a roundhouse kick to his head. And then from there, the knife was dropped, and he obviously came with us, and we had to walk him back right through the village back to our guys.

The Wild Journey

There were three of them in total, but he was the main one. We walked him back and he was charged and detained as a prisoner. That was a very successful day, so I remember that quite clearly.

But I guess what I'm basically saying is all these actions, all these smells, these feelings, this exposure that I was going through. What I didn't realise at the time was that I was being rewarded with something far, far more than all this – that when I was going to be returning back to Australian soil, I would be returning with PTSD, post-traumatic stress. This was going to change my life for a long time, a very long time.

See, a traumatic situation is one thing, but when you're doing it for an extended period of time, month after month, day by day, in a high, high-risk situation of casualties and death, that's not going to end well. We got awarded with an ICB badge and infantry combat badge, which the government statistically worked out based on how many days in conflicts, injuries, and loss of life you dealt with. You've got to basically be in a war zone to receive that badge. I was also awarded the Active Service Medal.

I came back to Australia, and I remember filling out a form on which one of the questions was, "Do you think you need psychological help?" I ticked yes. And when I got back, back onto Australian soil, we got put on leave and I went home back to Brisbane. There was no psychiatric evaluation, there was no nothing. I went home with far more than what I thought I was going to take out of doing operational service overseas. The problem was embedded and kept getting worse from that point on because my aggression level was insane. I was meant to meet my girlfriend at the airport that day, returning from Somalia, but I didn't want anything to do with her. I was cultured into being with the boys; I was cultured into being highly aggressive. I was

Deployment

heightened. I was full of adrenaline. I was 19 and just pumped up and now I was being sent back to Brisbane to go on holiday.

When I got back my mum said that I did the strangest things. She told me that I would sleep in all sorts of strange ways. She'd find me sleeping like a dog at the front of the door curled up. She'd find me asleep half hanging off the lounge; she'd find me asleep in the kitchen on the floor. I pretty much would sleep anywhere. And she said when she came into the bedroom, I would be there wide-awake staring back at her. Like there was nothing going on in my head, nothing said. I should have been asleep, and it freaked her out and she didn't know what was going on. I would often wake up in sweats. I also stopped calling my mum "Mum". I lost friends and relationships, I gained friends and relationships, but things changed dramatically from there.

I spent another year in the defence force because I'd signed up for four years, but I did five with the proviso that they were going to put me on courses that they never did. They were full of shit. They promised me things they didn't deliver. And I said I wanted out because when we got back, we were all treated badly. Other battalions disliked us because they didn't get deployed and were looked down upon by us for that alone. There was no budget in the army after this time, so I just said enough is enough. I was sick of throwing rocks at each other up in the back saying they were grenades and playing like kids in the sand pit. Because I'd seen the real thing, and what we were doing wasn't real. I couldn't distinguish going back to playing fantasy games that I did when I was a kid leading up to going into the army, I was past all that.

And some of the people coming into the army at that point in time, oh my God. It was the start of a new generation of completely different people. Some guys didn't even know how to start a fire. Some guys had never slept in a sleeping bag before. and I just couldn't fathom it. I couldn't adjust, I couldn't get used to these new guys. From there it became a whole new statistic, a whole new way of life and so I got out with the proviso that I had a job to go to. And that's how I made my way into the security industry and from the security industry, I went into all levels of different security. It was different going from a military background into a privatised job but for me, that was the start of a major problem that was going to have a huge impact on my life.

If you ever want to learn or read more on the Australian involvement in deployment to Somalia, there are plenty of books out there. Two great reads are Through Aussie Eyes and Chasing Bandits in the Badlands both written by Bob Breen. These books will give you a much greater depth of what I encountered along with others.

Chapter 4

CIVIL LIFE

The day came when I finally packed my bags and left my military career, my military lifestyle, what had been my way of life for years, and wow, what a ride, what a wild journey that was. Now I was starting a new journey into another world, a world I once knew. Now came the time when I would be transitioning from being a soldier, with a military lifestyle and military career, to a civilian lifestyle I left when I was just 17, a kid.

At this point in time in my life, I'd developed a relationship with a young girl up in Townsville. And I'd been contemplating for some time now that I just wanted to just settle down, I just wanted to move back to Brisbane and start a family. She originated from Brisbane as well, so it worked out quite well for both of us. We both wanted to start a family, have kids, and create change in our lifestyle. I didn't want to sleep out under the stars on the hard ground using a rock as a pillow, and no more waking up to

The Wild Journey

machine guns going off at 2am. I wanted to go home and be in a bed every night, you know, a comfortable bed, not have to be sleeping there with river rats crawling on top of my chest and falling asleep. Because, you know, I'm in Tully Far North, and it's raining, there's no dry spots, so for a river rat, the warmth of my chest to sleep on is bliss.

Her and I both shared a military background, which was kind of a comfort going into something new but sharing that connection. What people don't understand is that when you get out, there's no support. Well, there was no support back then. None at all. Back in 1996, there was zero. So having a partner knowing what I had been through and did, really helped a lot. I got out and was thrown to the wolves.

This relationship soon fell apart. The girl I was with fell pregnant and bolted out the door. I suspected for some time back in the army that when I was out bush, she along with many women up there was playing hide the sausage when I spent weeks away. There are a lot of gross things some women did up there. Most women attached to the army guys did not have good hygiene or ethics. One of many examples was the codes they used. Yes, codes. They would leave items on a window ledge for the guy they were cheating with. Things like AJAX, which meant army jerk at exercise. Or OMO, which was old man out. Pretty crafty right? Well, I suspected she was banging other guys and to this day I have no idea whose kid it is, maybe she doesn't either. So, I went and did security work.

I worked for a security company. It was okay. You know, it was nothing too fancy. I worked for another one that did concerts and VIP protection for artists and property. So that was quite cool, meeting famous people, getting to experience all that, being at the forefront of mosh pits, and grabbing people as they are thrown onto the stage or into the pits.

Doing personal bodyguarding, VIP protection, and property protection was another big role. One job I remember having to do often was pulling up in my car, and I'd spend a whole shift just watching a wall because the wall used to get graffitied and this guy used to have so much money that he could afford to have someone sitting in the car out the front of the wall outside his house to make sure no one graffitied it. This job was known as Wang's Wall.

I developed my interest in the security industry, and as the course of this employment went on, I also educated myself and got a Cert IV in private investigations. I created my own business, Kiril Investigations, and mainly did surveillance work with some fraud recovery. What an eye-opener that was. From police officers torching their own cars for insurance claims to cheating partners to name a very few things. There were a lot of stories, but that's another one for another book. Anyway, that was an interesting line of work as well. I stayed within the security industry till 2000.

I started to reach out and grab my own clients to do surveillance work and the cover work which was really quite good, and I did actually enjoy it. I had the decked-out vehicle that was all equipped with certain bits of technology back then. Certain man made stuff to help me carry out the surveillance work. So, it was quite interesting. But what was happening in the meantime in the security industry, was that I was discovering my high-volume aggression, especially in relationships – I was finding it very difficult to hold on to them. One of the key factors was always pulling in the wrong type of person as a partner in my

The Wild Journey

relationships, and these people, often enough, would either cheat on me behind my back, or they would just not communicate with me and cause me to get irritable and get aggressive. I would go from zero to 100 with aggression, not in the physical sense of hurting or hitting anyone, but more in the verbal aspect.

But at this point, you know, I really needed help and to learn what was going on within me. There were things boiling up inside of me that were only going to get worse. I started looking down on people when I got out of the Army because I had been obviously reprogrammed in the army to do so. And that's what they do. They reprogram you to be a soldier. Follow directions, don't ask questions, just do it. I was perfect for anyone who wanted to employ me for a job because I would always turn up on time, I'd be professional, and dress immaculately. And I'd carry out the task with no fear, I would just go and do it. But the problem was that I was developing side effects. And one of them was that I looked really down on people as civilians. I didn't see myself as an equal. I didn't see myself under these people. I saw myself in the pecking order above these people. And I had no respect, absolutely no respect for a lot of people. And I especially had no respect for women. This was a big problem. I'd been reprogrammed to see women as one thing in the army. So again, you know I wasn't given any help, I was given no instructions on how to deal with this. This situation, being in the security industry, stuff like that got worse. This went on until the year 2000.

I stayed where I was living at that time and met another girl. Again, she was way too young for me in the sense of a maturity level. I had just matured so much that even though I looked young, and really was still young, my maturity level in my brain had advanced. I was thinking more maturely than a person my

Civil Life

age. You know, if you go back and think about it, you look at today, how many 19-year-olds are overseas, being put in a position of a male adult having to make life decisions, not only their own but about their mates next to them and other people in a foreign country. I mean, most 19-year-olds are still popping pimples on their face and living at home with their parents.

From there, I moved in and out of a few relationships. There was no stability, I'd hold on for a few years in one relationship, bounce, and then have another one. Just no stability whatsoever. And then I finally met someone who later on became the mother of my two daughters, Charlie, and Kelsey, back in 2000. This year I was also stepping out of security and back into local government. I just managed to take a step out of the security industry. I'd had a gut full of it, I was spent dealing with grubs, and it wasn't doing me any favors with my behavior, being in an aggressive role.

What I decided was that I needed to do something a little bit more constructive, something a little bit more challenging, something a little bit more educational. I wanted to keep growing and being smarter. I wanted to become something much more and own my own business. They say it takes two years for the average soldier to adjust back into society when they get out of a military environment, and that was back in 1996. I don't know what it's like these days, but that's exactly how long it took me, two years to adjust and stop having nightmares and dreams and stuff like that, relating to the army.

I was still having horrible dreams where I'd wake up in sweats. Like I'd been dunked in a pool and jumped straight into the bed. I was having a lot of trauma. A lot of things were happening to me; I was being very forgetful. I'd forget where I put the keys to my car and stuff like that all the time, every day. There were a lot of underlying things that were happening that I still wasn't aware of. Things were bubbling away under my skin and in my brain. I was coming undone.

chapter 5

TOXIC

This is probably the most important chunk of my life that I've experienced to date. When I finally left the security industry, I would roll back into government, but this time all the way down the scale – into local government this time, remembering I first started off in Commonwealth Government as a soldier. I was now going to the bottom end of the government, and the bottom end indeed it is.

Now, look, everyone's going to have views and opinions on governments, and everyone's going to have views and opinions on what goes on inside governments. But this is my story. This is what I experienced, and it's something that many others inside governments have experienced as well.

It began back in 2000. I got recruited into local government, within Brisbane, and I signed up for an enforcement role. Again, that's pretty much all I really kind of knew and was great at. Now, at the same time, I just started a relationship that would soon evolve and turn into a marriage, from which I would have two daughters.

The story begins where I was recruited, and I remember sitting there and you don't remember, having very little to no use of computers. So, I went into Council HQ and sat in a chair, and I had to sit behind a computer to use Word. I didn't even know what Word was; I'd never used a computer till now. That's right, till now.

I had to type up a report. I'd never typed up a report before; I'd never done anything like that. My reports in Security were always handwritten and photocopied. Sometimes you just need to fake it to make it in life, and this was that moment. See, I knew I was a fast learner and able to think quickly under pressure thanks to my army background. But, you know, you've got to be careful because if you fake it too much, you will fall harder than most.

So, anyway, I crashed the computer and said I lost the document. A guy came over and set it all back up for me and said the computers were having issues. I had no idea what to say and just typed the report. I later sat through the interview processes of a panel of three different people and asked a lot of questions.

And then they put me out on the street and the first thing I did there was become a parking officer, or narc, as people like to call it, and it's pretty much the truth. I would go out there and deal with parking infringements, and regulate parking, to keep the city functioning and keep it moving to make it fair for other people to find a space. I could see value in that, and I could understand the principle behind it. I thought this job was not too bad because when I joined, I was given a car, a government car that I could take home, but I could only use it to and from work. I couldn't use it to go down to the Gold Coast and have a weekend and drive around the mountains. Still, I got a car which was a huge thing.

I was given everything. I was given a watch, socks, notepad, pens, uniform, boots, and a voice recorder. The list goes on and on. The only thing I really needed was underwear. And the money was really good, and the super was really good. The rostering was pretty good as well, it wasn't too bad at all.

I started off in the city itself in what they call the headquarters or the main office. There were only a few of us, but even that was too many. Some of us were going to have to go, and some of us were obviously going to stay on. I remember I worked my butt off, which we had to. We had a quota of infringements to reach each day. I was told, "This is a business, and we need to make money". They have revenue, they all do, including the police force – they all have revenue, and they have a quota. They can call it whatever they want, but it exists.

I had to go out there and get so many tickets per day, and I'd be questioned on it if my tickets were low. We had to write tickets and unfortunately what was happening and what still happens is that you've got people in those roles who are just gung-ho – they just love giving tickets, and they get off on it. You would think they are getting a commission on it the way they get excited. I've seen it with my own two eyes, and I've heard it with my own two ears. They absolutely get off on giving tickets to people, even to the point where they'll see someone coming down the road, make out they don't see them, and still write the ticket

The Wild Journey

and go, "Oh, I'm sorry, I've already printed the ticket". There's so much bad behavior in that particular role.

Anyway, I thought I was pretty straight, and I thought I was pretty fair with how I dealt out the tickets. I did what I had to do, but I was fair about what I did as well. I had morals you know, and that became relevant later because my morals kicked in and played a huge part eventually in my departure from this toxic place.

You know it wasn't long after I'd survived this role that I was offered another role in the city to allow me to stop being a parking narc. You all start off as a parking officer because that's the bread and butter and that's the crux of your job throughout your whole career in that area of enforcement, and so I then got into a small selection or a small team of people where we multitask and do different roles. We'd go out and do sentiment complaints, backyard burning, dog attacks, illegal signage, barking complaints and so much more. The list just goes on and on and on. I had to enforce the local and bylaws, and eventually, it wasn't too long before I actually was quite good at my job.

I actually got offered an opportunity to go to one of the four regions. Aside from central, which is its own region, there was south, west, east, and north region. Now, the south region was the closest to me because that was on the south side of Brisbane. And it was broken up into suburbs and my role was to enforce and regulate those areas of coverage. I was out in the south region for quite some time and conducted a more enforcement role in animal management, rather than parking. I was part of an animal management team. That's what they basically referred to it as. You would do some parking complaints, truck complaints, all that sort of stuff as well. But your primary role was animal enforcement, which was made up mostly of barking dogs, wandering dogs, and dog attacks – those were your three major ones. The team I was working with was an amazing little group of people that I clicked with very well. I had a great female leader – I had not worked under a woman before, ever. This was my first time. This woman Karen was truly a great leader. She was firm and fair. I always say there's a difference between a boss and a leader. A boss is just a person appointed to a position and works the job and nothing much more. And a leader is someone that you will follow, you'll look up to, and admire. Some people in life are born leaders, some people become really good leaders, and then others should just stay away from a position over people. Unfortunately, in local government, you do get a lot of bosses.

So anyway, I stayed there for quite some time and managed to do my job quite well. I never really had many hassles or anything like that. I had one guy, a Dutch guy, who was the supervisor out there at one point and he was just his own problem. In that business, there were people we could refer to as crawlers or brown noses and he was obviously one of those. I distinctly see those people because they were the ones that would climb their way up into higher job roles or better job opportunities, and I would get shoulder tapped.

If there is one thing I learned about local government it is that it's very ancestral, hugely ancestral. Someone's brother's mother's son's daughter's husband works there and you need to be really careful what you say because you don't know who you're talking to. They all cover each other's asses, something which eventually came to a head. There ended up being a huge external investigation into local government in our area, with workplace bullying the crux of it. It was investigated and people got stood down. I remember seeing people being served paperwork because they were under investigation.

So, what basically happened from there was that there was an opportunity for people to come into local government and they wanted people with obvious ethics. At the same time though, they wanted people with more enforcement role experience, so naturally they started introducing ex-police officers into the roles. Once they had one foot in the door, a whole lot of them started coming through and the next thing you know it was like an early retirement fund for them. We had all these coppers sitting in there that couldn't make it through the police force for whatever reason, and then they started to dictate their enforcing language.

Sadly, they saw the council as an early retirement fund and just looked at ways that they could easily make money and get paid holiday leave whilst turning this job into a police role. We got shuffled around, and Campbell Newman got in as Mayor and was meant to ensure the council wasn't too top-heavy – he needed to thin out unneeded roles. Instead, he created more job roles for management and thinned us out with more working roles and no extra pay. We lost vehicles, and positions – we were shuffled to regions far from home.

He was restructuring the restructured and redeveloping the redeveloped and there was a restructure on top of a restructure. It just kept going on and on. They kept shuffling us around like pawns – we were actually moving in areas in the same building almost weekly at one point. People were stressing out and becoming sick. They had a rapid response group that was like police officers, then they started segregating us and dividing and conquering us internally which then made us territorial within our own groups. This posed a problem because what was happening was this whole council was becoming toxic. It was already toxic to start with, but it now was hugely toxic, rife with narcissism and egos. Things that were going on in the council were absolutely fucking disgusting and I still cannot mention a lot.

Once these ex-police officers came in there was a huge drop in happiness in the workplace. People were stood down and forced out of their jobs. People were picked on and bullied. There were people who were paid to leave. It was really disgusting the behavior and what I saw going on. It was nothing short of just toxic and so I saw this and I was involved in this, and it was wave upon wave upon wave of attacks. The sad thing is our union did nothing; we had people, including myself, pulling out of the union because there was just no union there. There were just guys there collecting your $12 a week or whatever it was, and they were doing nothing with it. We look now in 2022 and we can see the government and how it treats its people; the way it bullies and coerces people into things. I mean you can only keep the lid on so long until it pops open and reveals the truth.

I ended up being moved to the west region. I was living in Jimboomba at that time, where I bought a property. I was commuting from there but then eventually I got forced to work in the north region. It was hell traveling every day, but I did it. They put me into another team as they had most of their team already structured in the north region. For me to be a part of this team I had to have my Cert IV in government investigations; luckily, I had completed this during my time in council. With this, I was able to go there instead of going over into animal management which was terrible because all you were doing was dealing with barking dogs' complaints and parking complaints. I was becoming a part of what they called a dog attack team, and my primary role was to be a senior investigator in these attacks across Brisbane. Causing fear and alarm constituted an attack so you can imagine there were a lot of dog attacks in Brisbane. There was a lot on my screen, but there was hardly anything under 40 investigations. There were also KPIs. We eventually got shuffled again and then we went into Fortitude Valley from where we set up and that was my home until I left in 2014.

While there I was part of a six-person team, and it was being in this team that led up to that point where I totally shut down and had my longest, darkest day.

I put up with so much shit in that place. We were often just given unreasonable tasks in unreasonable areas; I'd worked in Inala for two years in the south region and I had no issues in there even though it was as rough as guts – I saw a lot of things in there and dealt with a lot of problems and a lot of problem people, but nothing like this with my own team. I was very thankful that I met a great guy, Brad, who later left for another job for the same reasons as me. Just like the army we had each other's back and made a day great by laughing things off. I am still good mates with this top guy.

The problem was that internal, local government just basically has this thing that when you sign up you throw your heart and your soul in the little waste bin, and you get a knife in your back. When it will be twisted is anyone's guess, but it's only a matter of time. It's what they do, and I have seen people right at the top get taken down because they became a threat to another's position. When they have used someone, and they've had enough of them, they move them out.

Toxic

I remember one lady, an ex-copper, who was obviously a female in a male-dominated environment. She was good at a job - I'll give credit where credit's due – but then she started standing on toes because she became a threat. There were other people in senior roles that were threatened by her, thinking that she was going to end up taking their roles, and she probably could have. She started to really get vocal and really started standing up for herself and then one day, out of the blue, bang – gone. Where did she go? Well, it was that time where they came up and they took that knife, and they twisted it in her back. Suddenly she wasn't showing up to work, and no one ever heard from her again.

That's what they do. I remember when I was going through my investigations and made formal complaints on their behavior, their conduct, their ethics. I remember even the head person in charge of that area wrote me an email and started bullying me in the email. I screenshotted and showed people in the HR team and said look at this, how can officers learn any good ethics when you've got this coming from the top end. So much toxicity in local government. I would just do my job, and put my head down, but I just felt like it was just like there was a ton of bricks on top of me every day. Everything there was just micromanaged, everyone's watching someone instead of doing their bloody job.

I've seen so many things in there, but one thing that made me the sickest was the day I saw pictures of dogs, real dogs that we dealt with, on my supervisor's desk, and they had their eyes etched out with little crosses. These little crosses represented the dog's death and this supervisor who was in charge of our group, our coordinator, was actually getting off actually encouraging us to take dogs and put them down. I even got questioned one day about why I hadn't seized a dog yet. Often

The Wild Journey

when that happens the dog is put down. That's someone's pet, a part of their family.

I did my job effectively without having to do that. They eventually put the fencing up and did the right thing in the end. They may have taken a little longer, but they'd do it eventually. I got results and so this is where the conflict happens, this is where the problem lies, and this is where you see poor ethics. 14 years of my life I spent there and each and every day just got worse and worse and worse till I just had to go. I can tell you; I've never looked back ever since. You build this thing in your mind that there's nothing else out there, no other jobs, no other way of life, thinking that you'll never get another job. But I can tell you now, I've moved on to better pastures and is it greener on the outside of the fence? Absolutely it is, 100%. You know, I've worked in the city, better known as the concrete jungle or the zoo. It was a tough gig, but at the same time, was the best thing I did in order for me to learn and grow for my future.

chapter 6

MARRIAGE

In this chapter, I talk about my relationship, my marriage, and my children. The year 2000 was a pivotal point in my life as I'd gone back into government and started a relationship with a woman I would soon marry and have two children with. How we met was quite unique. When I was going through my recruitment process in the local government, I met up with another fellow who was an ex-firefighter, and he wanted to go out for a few drinks after work. He did like his alcohol a little too much as he was turning up drunk at training. I wasn't a drinker; I was pretty into my fitness, so I was pretty fit at that stage. He took me to a couple of pubs and clubs that afternoon. It was a bit like a pub crawl as I really still didn't really know much of Brisbane at all because I'd left when I was just 17, so I really hadn't had the chance to explore and get to understand the areas of my hometown.

The Wild Journey

On this particular day, we went out to some seedy places. One was in Logan somewhere, and this place was referred to as an amateur strip club. I go in, and I mean we're talking about Logan Underwood here. This place no longer exists from my understanding. As it turned out though, this was the place where I met the woman who was going to be the mother of my two children. I liked her and she did have a little resemblance to Nev Campbell at the time. She also told me that she had two daughters aged 3 and one turning 4. I wasn't worried too much as I had dated a woman before who was pregnant with another man. Anyway, most men would have run but I didn't, I asked if I could see her again and we made a further date to meet.

She lived in a place called Eagleby. People who know of this area would not dare drive through it with the windows down I later found out. Surprisingly, I lived in two houses over time in Eagleby and I only ever had a pair of shoes stolen from the front door. People there keep to themselves unless you put your nose into their business and then you have a problem. But, again, it's about public perception.

I went around her house to meet her for the first time outside of a club environment. I knocked on the door knowing she had kids. I went inside and there was a friend of hers there, which I thought was pretty inappropriate because it was supposed to be like a first date type of thing, you know? And I remember she was chopping up pot at the table with this woman, with no attempts to try and dress up – she was in a sarong. I remember I met the girls, Jaimee, and Alicia. Alicia came around the corner looking like a Chucky doll that rolled in vegemite or something like that. The kids were kids but come on, if you are meeting someone and investing in keeping a relationship make some efforts, right? I remember that day she was eating an apple and

Marriage

hurled the apple from one room to the kitchen. The charm, right? Cause that's what you do on a first date right? And kids hanging off the table as the pot was being chopped and smoked, fuck me. The situation was a mess and I thought oh my god she probably could have cleaned up the kids a bit and probably shouldn't have had her friend there but then to top it off, she was sitting at the table with drugs. Man, what was I thinking? But anyway, for the strangest of reasons I didn't walk. There was something within her that appealed to me through all that I saw. I still don't know what it was, but I stuck around so much that eventually I moved in.

At that point I was living in Albany Creek with a friend of mine, who was a copper. Once I moved in, it wasn't too long before we got a rental up the road, still in Eagleby, where we stayed for some time. It was pretty good; it wasn't a bad little place. It was there at this location that I later asked her to marry me. While we were there, we saved up to get our first home together as we wanted to have more kids. This was a tiny rental and not where I wanted to live for a long time. We ended up getting our first house just near the water at Loganholme, I remember we got it super cheap at the time. We moved in with four of us, and without too much waiting around, it ended up being that there were five of us. She had fallen pregnant with my first baby, our first daughter together named Charlie. Charlie was my first and the third for her.

We stayed there for some time. I remember I was living next door to these people, what you would call neighbors from hell. They were not there from the start. They came not long after we bought – there was a lot of movement in the area with buying homes as they were super cheap. I'd be trying to raise my kids and then this clown next door would just yell and scream at all hours of the night and morning any day of the week. And I mean not just here and there and occasionally, every friggin night. This clown had a dart board near our house where his entertainment area was, and he watched football and drank with his mates. Seriously it was that close, and he was a football nut and would watch football all the time. They never seemed to work and did very little. I later found out it was his mother's place, figures.

His mother lived up the road, and he got to the point I was getting that upset the police wouldn't do anything. I'd be making noise complaints on a weekday before work at around three o'clock in the morning. There was screaming, fighting, music and on one occasion the breaking of glass doors and beer bottles on the road, it was just disgusting. Here I am trying to raise young kids and work. I had to put up with that for quite a few years; this was my house, and I was going to fight this. My PTSD was through the roof at this point. One day they pissed on my dog through the fence, and I was done. The cops were useless, so I was just about ready to hook a rope to my towbar and noose it and drag him through the fence and along the main road. If he could scream after that he was a miracle baby. This was my home.

So, I was dealing with that whilst I was working with council right. This was going on in the background, and then I started to discover a couple of little things which didn't make sense with my partner at this time as well. She was working in a bar down the road since 2000 and she would come home in the early hours having done night shifts. She would clean out the back of the car in the early hours of the morning and I'm like, you never clean the car. You know, like there were all these little things, like smoking habits and stuff like that. She said

Marriage

she didn't smoke but she'd go outside and hang a jacket on the clothesline first thing when she came in through the house and obviously, I suspected that she'd been doing recreational drugs. I later found out her previous partner, and the father of her children was Australia's most wanted Ponytail bandit. See, she lived a shady past and once said to my mum, "If he knew some of the things I did, he would not marry me". And that part started to seep out. You can keep a lid on things for a few years, but eventually, it comes out. Things started to surface, and I started to see fragmentations of the relationship, but silly me, I continued with this woman.

We ended up marrying and had a beautiful garden wedding at Mount Cotton. It was really beautiful, and we had a nice bunch of people to help celebrate the moment. After the wedding, we eventually went on a little honeymoon retreat for a few nights. Nothing big, just kept it quite simple. And then my little monkey Kelsey came along. Kelsey was conceived and, like both my children, born at the Logan hospital. I remember the day before Kelsey went into the hospital, I remember nesting. I was in the garden and through the house, tidying everything up, and was really particular with things to the point of even zip-tying all the fiddly cables behind the TV together. I was being really anal about everything. And then later that night the water broke, and Kelsey came into the world really quickly. We just got to the hospital and her head was already out in the waiting room.

And that was the beginning of my relationship with my two beautiful daughters. What happened from there is we ended up deciding to sell our home and move away from the toxicity of the clowns next door. It was getting too much for me, causing me to drink a lot more as well. So, I said let's get some acreage, I'd like to get away and not be close to people like this anymore.

The Wild Journey

I'd like to have a bit of space and I'd like to be able to give the kids an opportunity to experience things that normal kids in suburbs often don't. Things like having chickens and watching baby chickens hatch. Have a dog run around on this property, you know, all these things that they can't do in the residential zone. We decided for the sake of affordability that we'd move out to Jimboomba.

We found a nice block on two acres, and we ended up building a home through a building agency and getting it all designed the way we wanted it. It was really exciting. However, at this time we also found out that my baby girl Charlie had reflux. Basically, she was found to have one kidney where the urine was traveling back into it, and it had to be removed. Since she was born, she has had high fevers. Luckily our doctor was smart and knew what was going on and got onto it right away. My little Charlie had a few issues when she was born, and we were always up at the children's hospital in between work. So, our greatest fear was moving onto the property and having to live in a caravan or shed. We needed Charlie to be comfortable during this process. We had to stay a week at a rental property in Eagleby while our house was being built. It was so small for six people. But to be honest I had some really great times there. I had the best Christmas ever there. The only thing that sucked was the landlord overcharged us to have a contract week to week as we didn't know when the house would be ready. But we paid for it for the sake of my daughter's comfort.

We ended up taking a design and putting it on the block and it became our home for seven years. It was a great time, and it was reasonably peaceful. Having said that, there were a lot of unpleasant, strange people living around us and in the area. In fact, it was worse in these areas as a lot of misfits go further out

Marriage

because they cannot associate with normal people, or they get cast out through being disruptive. A lot have a mental illness like paranoid personality disorder. They would hide behind objects and watch you constantly. How did I know this? Later I became a firefighter in Jimboomba, and I got to know what was in my community better than the people themselves. And the police next door to the fire station told me, as they dealt with the problem directly.

I remember I had a guy who lived in his shed next to my bedroom window. He was a truck driver, he was an alcoholic and obviously, his wife didn't want him in bed with her. He used to sleep in the shed and would dance around with rum till the morning and then go jump in his truck and drive to work. Just bizarre. I was starting to discover that these sorts of things were being attracted into my life. I was thinking this is just uncanny; everywhere I go I'm pulling in all these friggin idiots, these clowns, these narcissistic, toxic, egotistical, drunk misfits in society. What was going on!! Why me? It became such a problem that I just couldn't understand.

I didn't realise at this point that there was something going on inside of me. There was something, a timer going, and the bomb was about to go off. By 2014, and I didn't realise this, my drinking had become more consistent. I wouldn't say that I was a chronic alcoholic, but the drinking was definitely becoming more consistent. I would isolate myself a lot more and was being forgetful, but I also had a partner there that was playing on this as well you know, using this to her advantage.

If it wasn't hard enough already, my wife's oldest daughter would always fight with me, almost like her mum. In fact, at one point she was looking like her mum and acting like her. It was creepy and odd. The problem was that the mother was always at the tavern when this happened and would come home, shut the door and me out and have a secret meeting. She was always protected. And I was always wrong. Eventually, the mother got to a point where her daughter would say that one of us had to go. It was too much. Often, I'd be on the phone at night saying you've got to get home, this is out of hand. I felt like I had two wives taking shifts on me, making me feel like a little kid. I was getting burnt out, and eventually, I just said, it's either me or her. One of us has got to go. I can't keep doing this. I started to come apart.

Her daughter eventually moved down south to live with the wife's mother, where she stayed. She'd come up occasionally for visits, but she stayed there. Then the second round was the second oldest daughter. She started getting older and she started challenging around the 16-year mark but this time the challenge was more with the mother. The mother and her would fight and bicker and argue every day without fail. The mother would just get up and just scream and fight and argue and carry on, and this just stuck in my head. We were all having to hear it, including my two daughters.

I would go off at this point in my life. I was becoming very aggressive, vocally aggressive, because it was frustrating. I was frustrated and being in a house full of women was just getting too much because I was going from working in the city all day to the fire station and home working on the property, then rinse and repeat. Sometimes I was doing overtime and callouts back-to-back.

I remember one day I was attending a suicide and had to go to work right after and deal with someone complaining about

Marriage

a dog barking, then go home and deal with issues there. I had no break. I was on autopilot. The marriage just depleted, it was now fuelled by so many lies and mistrust. The marriage was dead and so was I inside. The toxicity and lies piled up, and as it went backward and forwards I just couldn't keep up. The one thing I knew was that if I left the relationship my daughters would be used as a bargaining chip, and I wasn't going to get to see them. I was extremely close to my two daughters. I love and still love my two daughters Charlie and Kelsey with all my heart. Charlie at the age of two lost one of her kidneys and was always in and out of the hospital at a very early age and it absolutely destroyed me to see that little girl being put to sleep to go in and have something removed because she was so sick.

I ended up just saying to myself this needs to stop. This whole situation needs to stop now before I do something I cannot undo. My time was up. My internal bomb was about to go off. All the years of trauma and toxic situations had finally caught up. My mind, body, and soul were spent.

The wall was about to be hit with full force.

The Wild Journey

Chapter 7

PIN UP BOY

This chapter was thrown in as it had a significant part to play in my life leading up to my darkest day. This is actually more in detail about the two-year journey of being nominated and accepted in a fireman's calendar. Now, the reason I've decided to create a chapter on this is that it was a significant part of where I went, and where I was going. I believe things happen for a reason. This is one of those things.

I invested in the firemen's calendar for a few different reasons. One, in fact, was I felt really down about myself and depressed, I did not love myself and I thought I was quite ugly and disgusting. I couldn't even stand looking at myself in the mirror. I had no self-love, no self-worth. I was put down by my partner. I was told I always had a gut. I didn't have abs and yeah, she was not hot cake either. I kind of wanted to try and change that. I was going to apply for something that was definitely way out of my

The Wild Journey

reach and something that I'd never done before and that was to apply for this calendar.

This was back in 2014, and I was turning 40 that year. So ironically, I had my wife at the time take some photos of me in my turnout pants with my shirt off and oiled up with a fire stick. Turnout pants are those big yellow pants you see the fireman wear to fires. The photo was very tasteful, and I was a firefighter at the time, so I met the qualifications for this. But did I meet the look? So, I applied and submitted a photo.

And that photo, which I've put in the book, is the photo that got me into the fireman's calendar. Yes, I was told I got in. Now I was not super cut, I was not super lean or anything like that. It was just a goddamn good photo, and it was original, not done before. It's not all about abs, not all women want the same thing as I later found out. So that photo won me a spot in the firemen's calendar for 2015.

What happens is you go and do the photoshoots in 2014 for the release of the calendar for 2015, and then the 2015 photoshoots for the 2016 calendar, and so on and so forth. It's usually around April, around my birthday. So, I got this news, and I was super excited, really excited because it just lifted my confidence a little bit that someone actually saw potential, saw something in me that was amazing enough to put it in a calendar.

Then I started to train. This time, I had something to train for. It was amazing to actually get out there and actually have a goal and that goal was to be super fit and to look really good, and in turn, build my confidence and self-love and worth. Unfortunately, most would later see this as attention-seeking or worse still, ego. But they didn't know me and my journey.

Pin Up Boy

That's one thing with mental health, you often do not see it like a broken leg.

Now there's a little story behind the calendars. And I can't say too much, but I can say that at the time, the calendars had been run for many years by a particular individual. And he was a nice guy. He was a pretty good guy, he looked after me, and he looked after his boys, and he made sure we were doing a good thing and getting out there selling those calendars. The calendars were a big hit up and around the Ekka and we would do a lot of our sales to make a lot of money. And then a percentage of that would then go over to the Children's Burns Unit as charity to help them out.

I thought this was a damn good opportunity to get super fit out of this and build my confidence up, and I'm going to do a really good thing and help raise money for a really good cause. So, the journey began. I got super fit. And then I really started to focus on myself a lot. Now I couldn't go to the gym because I had two young kids and I had property and I had responsibilities. I was working pretty much three jobs if you want to consider looking after the property as well. I was working for the local government, the fire station and working on the property, as well as looking after my kids. Busy, busy, busy.

So, the day came, and we got our photoshoots done. We each got nominated for a particular month based on a review panel and photos. I got nominated as Mr. November for that particular year. And so, we went out and started selling calendars. You'd go around, and you'd sell calendars wherever you could. Back then you could go to markets, fairs, shopping centres, pretty much anywhere and everywhere and sell these you would get a lot of invitations to events to sell the calendars. The calendars were super cheap and very popular back then amongst women but not limited to just them. The first year the calendars were quite good, and I was quite successful at selling calendars and getting out there. I went to a lot of different places, got to see a lot of different things, got behind the scenes, and to be really, really honest, I felt like a rock star. I had privileges, I was given things for free. I'd never had so much attention in all my life. I had women just coming up to me left right and centre hitting on me, it was just full on, full on. If I'd ever experienced anything close to a rockstar lifestyle this was certainly it. And I enjoyed every moment. It was a once in a lifetime dream, every man's dream I'd say. But for me, it was going to be twice in my lifetime.

The second year I got accepted again and I became Mr. March for that year. But the second year, it started to really open up my eyes and things really took a turn for the worse. They say that everything that goes up must come down. Well, exactly right. In the second year, I was super fit, the fittest I'd ever been since the military. I was super fit. You know my body was cut; I was super strong. I had great muscles and abs. I was working out six days a week every week for nearly two years. And I felt fantastic. I felt so confident in my life. I'd never felt so much confidence ever in my life before until this point.

But while everything was looking quite good on the outside, on the inside everything was falling apart still. I hadn't managed my problem with my depression and anxiety and my DID, and Complex PTSD. The marriage was failing, too, and eventually did fail. And at that point in time, my local government job was getting worse. I was getting bullied; I was getting harassed more. And that was taking a toll too. I was getting really sick and tired of the fire station; the politics down there was absolutely disgusting. There were just so many negative things around my life. As for the calendars, a lot of crap was going on behind the scenes. There were those in the calendars that were barely firemen. I don't even think personally that some of them were firemen at all. They never came up in searches nor did any of the boys know of them – definitely they weren't known around the fire stations.

On top of that, there were people taking the money that was for charity in some cases. In some situations, the money wasn't even going to charity. It was going straight into people's pockets. It was being used for things like accommodation, drinking, food, and it wasn't even seeing itself in the charity bucket. I remember people putting their hands in the charity bucket and buying coffee with it. I was starting to see things that I was disgusted by, which made me realise how dodgy most charities are.

A different guy took over this business, and I was disgusted by him. He turned it into a business, and it was no longer a charity. You could feel the change and the money grab taking place from there on. Yeah, they put some money towards the burns unit because that helps promote the look and feel of something authentic and give the impression that they're doing something wonderful for someone else, but it's really just a money grab. Some of the things I overheard and saw were so wrong. The guy running it was nothing more than a Gold Coast thug in my opinion.

And the attention I got - eventually I got sick of it. Women started to show their true colors. It was bringing out all the nut jobs. I had females that were harassing me. I had females that were sending me videos and photos. I was hit on by young, old, black, and white. Professionals, such as police officers and lawyers, and of course married. It was just a dirty, seedy world

The Wild Journey

that I didn't want to be a part of anymore. Something that I saw in the first year as being wonderful turned out in the second year to be absolutely disgusting and I was done with people making up fake accounts trying to burn me, trying to psych me out. I was out. I was sick of it. All it was doing was bringing out desperate women and disturbing my mental health.

I couldn't handle that anymore; I wanted someone to like me for me. That's when I met my new partner, Jo. And Jo saved me. She pulled me out of that world. I pulled the pin on the calendars. I resigned, and I got out of it. I sold my last calendars at the shopping centre, and I walked away. I owed them nothing. They owed me nothing. That was the end of that, and I never went back to that garbage ever again.

I was always clear about any charity that was out there, there was always something seedy and dark about them. I didn't trust them, but Jo pulled me out. We met during the calendars in 2014 at a conference at supernova where we both were signing autographs. I was signing calendars and she was signing books from a movie as she was an actress. We met again later in 2015 in the second year, and we ended up dating and being together for a good six years. She got me through a lot and helped me through my mental handicaps. She was a savior, a blessing in disguise. And through her, I was able to give up drinking for six years straight without going to AAA or anything. I started getting on medication to help me control myself better. I started going to appointments with psychologists. Once I got away from the calendars, that's when I realised, I needed to get out of council, and my toxic marriage. Yes, I was still married and yes Jo did know. I was living under the same roof but in different rooms. The marriage was done, but not over. Oh no, it was far from over. My wife at the time was going to do what most nasty women do; make my life hell and hurt me through my back pocket and my children. This was still a huge change. This was massive.

When people say things happen for a reason, they do. I believe they do, and I believe I was meant to be in it for two years. To build my confidence, look good, and meet Jo. See, I manifested something different this time, something positive. That's how I was able to meet Jo. She was my savior, helping to get me out of that toxicity from all those people in all those places. She helped me recover and brought so much light to what was going on. There were and are so many who hated her for hanging in there and helping me. She didn't have it easy with me. I was broken and she had to rebuild me.

You can see the shift in my life, and how we draw in people and situations based on our own emotions, right?

The Wild Journey

chapter 8

DIAGNOSIS

We are now in 2014. This was an interesting time because, just pulling back a little bit from 2014 as we go back into it, what had happened was, I was turning 40 at the time so there were a lot of life changes. There were a lot of things happening in my life and they all seemed to be happening at once. As I say, if it doesn't rain, it pours and this is exactly what had happened, right?

Everything had been leading to this point in my life. This was what I call the crossroads. My marriage has failed and was depleted. There was no trust or love and hadn't been for many years in the relationship. There'd been nothing. It had just been a loveless relationship. During this process, leading up to just before 2014, when I moved out to Jimboomba, I started employment with the Queensland Fire and Rescue Service. Now I did the Queensland Fire and Rescue Service for a good six years. I was out there in Jimboomba as a rural and auxiliary firefighter. Our station was a hybrid of both. For those who don't know what that is, it's the same as what an urban firefighter does, same principles. You do the same things; you go out to house fires, car accidents, kittens up trees, all that stuff. You go out and you do education programs at schools and nursing homes etc. I was very fortunate that I was able to go out and educate my daughter's class, Charlie's class, and actually do a talk. I jumped in my turnout gear and talked about fire safety and stuff and had them jump on the big red fire truck. How many kids can say their dad was a firefighter and came out to the school with the big red truck and did a talk on fire safety and got to jump in the fire truck? I can say it was a pretty proud dad moment there.

So, I'd done that for six years, and obviously, I'd seen the loss of life and I'd seen people pretty messed up in car accidents, and I'd seen my fair share of house fires as well. So, you know, beyond other things I did I was also invested as a rural firefighter. We were on a paging service where we got paged to turn out instead of sleeping at the station.

I'd always wanted to be a firefighter. I think most boys do. I had always been in uniform roles most of my life, always roles of authority or roles of enforcement, roles of responsibility, and always pretty full on. I'd been doing that and as I said, I was exposed to quite a lot of things, traumatic situations over time. Exposure on top of exposure. I was often sleep-deprived because I was on a paging service. I had to be within a certain distance from the station to turn out and respond to a situation.

I was still working for the local government council at this point in time, and I was then going home to a toxic situation. Then I was going down to the fire station, which seemed all

Diagnosis

good for a while. It was great that I was going down there. It was an outlet for me to get away from home and council. But after a while, even the station became demanding, people were whining and bitching down there. So again, I was in another government role now.

At this point, I was working in local government as well as state government. And the consistent theme I saw throughout all these governments – no matter if it's local, state, or commonwealth – was the number of toxins coming from people and the situations within the house. You know, it doesn't matter what level of government you're working at. It was all cut-throat. Everyone is trying to climb on top of each other's backs to get things. Tapping on shoulder situations, bullying, sexual harassment, don't get me started on that. Men get harassed too, trust me. I even had a colleague grab my hand at my desk and place it on her boob and said how do my new boobs feel. Of course, she was married too. Everything that they preach, they don't do. It happens. It happens all the time. So very toxic. You've got to brown nose to survive, you know, they like you to grovel to get places. I was never one of them, and nor will I ever be, and I'm proud of that because I stand on my own two feet. I am what I am. I am who I am. I am me. I was no puppet. I was awake.

Basically, it just became this triangle. I'd go to my job in council, go home, work on the property and bust my ass off within a broken marriage. Then down to the fire station, toxic, toxic, toxic, toxic, toxic, toxic, this triangle of toxicity was just continuously surrounding me. And I was not getting anywhere. I was making great money, but I was spending the money and putting it back into the property, right? I wasn't getting anywhere. I was just working, drinking, and working. I had a boat, and I couldn't even get it out to go fishing. It was just madness. I had a female

The Wild Journey

lieutenant down there at the station who told me I couldn't go out of Jimboomba because they were relying on people to turn out in the fire truck. I did still have a life, but they said no, you can't leave Jimboomba today because we need you to be on call in case something happens. So here I was continuously waiting around for things to happen, right? And it was just insane. I wasn't even allowed to go out of my own area.

In one case, a gentleman hanged himself. I went out in the really early hours of the morning, and I had to be exposed to that, then from there, I had to then go to the local government job. And then I had to deal with a barking dog. Someone whining about a dog that barks too much. This whole thing was just getting crazier and crazier and crazier. And I was losing myself and I was spiraling. Then all of a sudden, I turned 40 and I said fuck it. I wanted to challenge myself. I didn't want to be like this. I reached out and I went and applied for the fireman's calendar.

Now by this stage, there were a multitude of different things happening. I started going to a counselor because of my relationship problem, and I was not coping, and I was done – I mean I was spent. I felt like I was going to do something really bad to someone.

I met this counselor, Deborah Brown. I've been to counselors before for marriage and relationship issues, and some of them were disgusting. Absolutely disgusting. All I can say is if you're going to counselors, psychiatrists, psychologists, you need to do your shopping and you need to look around because I can tell you 100% that some of them shouldn't be doing the job they do. I had one male counselor lean forward in a meeting that I had with my partner, my ex-wife. He leaned forward and said to me, you're the problem! Now, who does that? He was reported and

Diagnosis

I went to someone else. I went to one who would get her phone out and get you to watch YouTube clips of self-help. I had another one who specialised in military backgrounds, and he operated from home. I walked out halfway through. He didn't know what to do, he said I can't help you. But he took the payment with no problems. There were so many disappointments out there with these people in this industry who call themselves counselors, psychologists, and psychiatrists, which is very disappointing, but eventually I came across this one woman Deborah Brown at Jimboomba.

I went in to see her and told her what was happening in my life. I told her everything about my situation; my work situation, the fire station situation, firefighting, my marriage, everything including the army I laid on the table. And she just said to me, I think you might have PTSD. I knew of PTSD, and I'd suspected for many years that I had PTSD. I'd spoken to many veterans about PTSD. And they would tell me, especially Vietnam vets, about some of the symptoms that would go along with PTSD. Forgetfulness, irrationality, anger, outbursts, sweating in your sleep at night, not being able to sleep, and jumping at loud noises. I sat down and said I'd been trying to tell people that I had PTSD for a long time now, right back to when I was back in the Army overseas. And I was at the OP observation point, and I took that form saying I needed help. I knew something wasn't right with me back then. This woman said to me that she'd like to prescribe some medication through my doctor to obviously take away the anxiety and the depression because of what was happening to me.

At this point, my drinking had also increased. I was drinking a lot more than what I should have been. And I was passing out. I was having severe anxiety attacks and passing out and vomiting and I couldn't lift myself off the lounge or off the floor. I could barely walk some days because I had such bad depression. At some stage, I did think about ending my life and not just once. I was an absolute mess but somehow, for some reason, I kept on going to work, kept on going home, kept on going to the fire station.

Then I started the medication, and it did bring me down and did relax me a little bit more. It started to calm me down a little bit. At this stage it was on a mild dose but after I did more counseling and discovered more issues I had, I continued drinking with my medication on top of it. This was absolutely making things even worse because now when I had one beer, it was equivalent to having two or three because I was medicated. I wasn't controlling that; I was having blackouts. I couldn't remember a lot of what I did because of the blackouts now. And so, I wasn't aware of this, you know.

The calendar then had an adverse effect on me in the second year, plus I had my wife or ex-wife starting to sabotage my calendar work. She was getting people to jump on sites and connect with fans, connect with people, and sabotage me, telling people what I was like or what she portrayed me to be like. And so, I started to have people going against me now while I was being medicated and drinking. This was turning into a royal shit show.

What had started as a lavish lifestyle there for a year or so started to go downhill really, really quick. And it only takes a few people to see that you're succeeding and you're enjoying life and you're doing well to try and take you down; that's what we call tall poppy syndrome. So, I was being stalked. I was being harassed. I was being threatened. I was being intimidated. I was coping with all these things while already struggling mentally. I totally started

Diagnosis

to lose it. So, I pulled quietly out of the calendars and said fuck it. I don't want anything to do with corruption, theft and dishonesty, and a place where there's no ethics.

So, I let go and quietly parted ways.

By now I was also pulling back from the fire station and was about to pull out of council. This was the tipping point.

By this point I had just started seeing Jo, and I remembered what Deborah Brown said. If I continued to work in roles exposing me to trauma it would not result in a good outcome. I was advised to stop being a firefighter and give up council along with leaving the marriage. This was the start of a new beginning.

I often look back and see how hard I had to be shoved to move along, to go onwards and upwards.

Chapter 9

CROSSROADS

A lot happened in 2014, and this is what I refer to as my crossroads. This is when I started to fall apart, explode you might say. It was also the time that I actually started to rebuild myself. I reached the fork of the crossroads and I had to work out which direction I wanted to go. So going forward a little bit here. I obviously made the choice to quit the fire service after six years of service with the Queensland Fire and Rescue Service. I was done. One of the things that Deborah had said to me and that had stuck in the back of my mind was that with PTSD, it's very dangerous to continue what you're doing being in the fire service, and also dealing with negative people all the time in toxic situations like local government. What's going to happen is, there's going to be a time and a place where a smell, sound, color, or visual response is going to trigger you. It's not a case of it, but when. And when you're triggered, that could cause devastating effects. I could end up, and I hate to say it, considering suicide. I will adopt what they call exposure on top of exposure. This can result in complex PTSD. What I didn't know just yet was that I had it. I had from the military and childhood trauma. But that wasn't discovered yet.

See the situation I was faced with – now what was I to do?

I stopped with the firefighting and in turn the fireman's calendar, because obviously I have ethics and moral standards, and I just couldn't keep doing that as well. I started pulling back on things; I started to change things around. Now see at this point in time, I had also found a new relationship. Jo was a godsend. She was beautiful and very smart. But she wanted to help me, so she became a rescuer. This turned out later to be bad for her own health and well-being. Jo had a lot going for her. She was a teacher and actress, and she had a son named Beau. What we ended up both having was also ex-partners in a court of child custody arrangements. This was not exactly fun.

When I met her, I instantly fell in love with her. I did. I fell in love with her. And she fell in love with me. We hit it off. I truly did not love before her. I remember I was selling calendars, and I was at a shopping centre when I'd already met her. I'd met her at supernova. Just briefly she came over and got a photo with me and another fireman. She was there doing a promotional thing for a book, and she was signing and doing autographs and I was doing calendars and signing autographs. And then I came across her a year later at another shopping centre, just a shopping centre in the suburbs. And she stopped me and said, "Do you remember me?" I said, "Yeah, I do". I had asked her if she wanted to meet somewhere and have a coffee and you know, a date. Now at the same time, I was still living with my wife, but though I was under the same roof we were separated and living in two different rooms, which I now find out is quite common in a lot of relationships.

Crossroads

People just don't tell you and post lies on social media. A lot of people do that because they have children involved right? What I discovered is that this woman has come into my life for a reason.

Now see, one thing about me is I believe in fate, I believe in the universe. Okay, this is my spiritual side coming out of me now. This is where I have a moment where I go, the universe will prevail; it will provide and do what's needed to create balance for good or bad. And so, Jo came into my life. And she was like a rescuer. She hated the calendar, and me being in it, which I understood. She couldn't stand them. She could also see the toxicity in the local government with the council. She had seen that as well. She had listened to the recordings I had of the bullying and so forth. Those hidden cameras and voice activation devices really paid off. Remember I was an investigator. She also knew all about the fire station.

The only positive things I really had were my two girls, Charlie, and Kelsey. My daughters were my inspiration and motivation to do good. They were my comfort. They were my everything. Now I'd met Jo, and I met her son Beau, and it wasn't long until I'd moved house and taken up a rental property at Mount Warren Park. At this point I was going to start battling for my kids. Because what had happened was my wife had absconded with my two children and took off one morning. I remember getting up and giving my girls a bit of a hug and a kiss and going to get a coffee down the road, on a day when I would normally be going to work. But today I decided to take it off. I went down there to get a coffee, and when I came back, she had fled with my two girls to a secret location. And I didn't know where my girls were.

I put out an Amber Alert. I obviously had my concerns, and I didn't know where my girls were. I'd never been one night

The Wild Journey

without my girls and talking to them, at least saying I love them. So, between Jo and I we spent a good week doing a bit of investigation work. And we ended up finding where my two girls were. In the meantime, my solicitor called me and said I had done the wrong thing by using social media to raise attention for my daughters. The women, in that firm, were useless. Fantastic at taking my money and that was it. I later sacked her and represented myself in court. As I said to her before parting ways, "At least I did something and got results". And it's also funny how the universe provides things to you. Because I went to the bank one day, and we had a joint account and wanted to close it obviously. And the bank flagged up on the screen her residential address and the lady said do you live at XYZ? I went hmm, no, that must be her address. And so, she took it down, but I'd already obtained what address it was, and I remembered it and I quickly wrote it down. That's how I found out where the kids were actually living but I kept that a secret, and I kept that to myself in case of an emergency. But, you know, I had to jump through hoops to see my two daughters, and that was devastating, absolutely devastating. Not just for me but for my girls because they were ripped out of their school, their swimming club, their friends, their dad, their home, their beds, their environment. They were totally ripped out of everything because someone was being selfish and wanted to punish me.

Jo took me on a path to help me, and better myself. There were a lot of things that needed to be done. There was a lot of work ahead. And one of the things was I had to get out of council; I had to get out of the government. I'd gotten rid of the fire station. I'd gotten rid of my toxic relationship and next I had to get rid of the job that I'd had for 14 years. I had to get rid of it. And that's when the whole thing came to a head because that day I sat in that office, and it was the longest, darkest day in my life.

Crossroads

So, I did it. I got out of the matrix and broke free and went on stress leave, sick leave. Now fortunately for me, I did have quite an accumulation of sick leave because I worked in local government, and I had never-ending sick leave. So, with HR checking in on me I was still getting paid which was great. I started to sit back with my time, and I started to think about what I am going to do. I needed to do something here. I needed to fix this, right? Jo said to me, well, you need to stop drinking. It was causing problems and a lot more because I was on medication. It really honestly was causing a lot of problems.

I tried to stop drinking on my own, I tried it but fell off the wagon a lot of the times as the stalkers would put it. I was being stalked and harassed, and I had my accounts hacked and everything like that. I was having my stalkers tell me that I'd fallen off the wagon like they were watching and hearing everything I was doing, which was amazing. But then one day, one day, it came to me. My daughter had put in a statement for court. Kelsey, my youngest daughter, said, "Every time I look at Dad, he's got a drink in his hand. Dad's always drinking." That made me think, is that the legacy I want to leave when I depart this planet? I didn't have a drink in my hand 24/7, but that's what my daughter perceived. That's what she saw. She didn't see anything but that. I had to fix that; I had to stop.

So, the journey began, and with the help of Jo, I stopped drinking. I was just doing it. No AA, I wasn't using any other medication. I wasn't doing anything other than just going cold turkey. And yeah, I went through withdrawal symptoms. Oh my god did I go through withdrawal symptoms. It was like being an addict. Well, I was addicted to alcohol. I was going through sweats. I was going through uncertainty. I felt like shit. I felt like I was losing my personality, I felt like a part of me was missing. That was scary, because I was always creative and always inventing things and coming up with stuff, and I believe that the alcohol was a part of that thing to get me into that mindset. I thought God, without it I'm going to end up nobody, so it was playing tricks on my mind. It took a good month to stop that thought pattern.

I was also told it takes three months before you actually stop thinking about alcohol altogether. I'd go to the beach and go man I could do a cold beer. I would drive past and catch the eye of the pub and think it would be nice to sit out there and have a cold beer. And this kept happening but eventually, one day it just stopped, I stopped thinking about it. And then lo and behold, I stopped drinking. In fact, I stopped drinking completely for six years, not a drop. No relapse, no nothing. Six years. I stopped drinking, and the only person that made me do that was my youngest daughter with that comment, and Jo being persistent with me. We started to deal with the alcohol problem. And I was getting on top of it, and I was winning. I also noticed that I was saving money as well. I started to see a shift in friendships. I lost toxic people around me and replaced them with talented souls.

But then there were still other issues that were starting to surface because one thing was being cleaned up, and another thing was starting to show up. And one of the things was that I had other addictions, one of which, with the assistance of alcohol, was a sex addiction. I needed to deal with that. Because through all the infidelity, and all the trauma from everything in my life, I could obviously get my endorphin hits via sex. It was unhealthy what I was doing, so I needed to fix that.

I started to get help along with Jo, she helped me get into SA six, sexaholics anonymous and I became a part of that circle of men to fix it. There's no embarrassment about it because I wasn't doing anything illegal or anything like that. I just had a sex addiction. Plain and simple; pornography was my issue. I just needed to escape and that was my escape. What I was starting to learn was alcohol and this addiction was my escape, they were my coping mechanism. I needed to obviously stop escaping. While dealing with this I also started to think outside the box, and started thinking what other job can I do? Because I couldn't do anything that's going to trigger me, I couldn't do anything that was going to cause problems.

I'd now identified that I had PTSD. I'd now identified that I had a drinking problem. I'd now identified that I had a sexual addiction. I had depression, I had anxiety, and I was afraid. And I realised I had all these different things happening because, the joy of having PTSD is you get all these wonderful things, all these defects with it. It's wonderful. It's amazing, so blessed – not. I had to fix this because this wasn't going away. I then got into a couple of different counselors, and I started to see a couple of different psychologists, looking at a view of trying different treatments. I'd had enough of different views and ideas, I wanted to know once and for all on the record, did I or did I not have PTSD? Because if I did, the military is responsible for that because it stems back to when I was deployed in the service, and they need to be responsible for that. You can't just throw someone out and just leave them wounded. And unfortunately, there are a lot of wounded soldiers out there that aren't even in the army anymore that are suffering from this and more.

I had to find someone, and then eventually I found Dr. Ruth Armstrong, an amazing woman. I went to her and when I went to her, I absolutely broke down, I totally lost my shit and cried my eyes out. I just bawled my eyes out. And I just told her everything. I was not coping well. So, with my own money, my own time, and my own pride, I went ahead and got her to do all these different evaluations on me. I can't remember how many evaluations she did on me, but there was a lot of paperwork and physiological tests. What we found next was shocking.

Not only did I have PTSD, but I had Complex PTSD. Now for those who don't understand what Complex PTSD is, that is exposure on top of exposure. Now this stems from having been in the military, combined with the fire service, but also going all the way back to childhood trauma. So, I had a multitude of things. It's the worst PTSD you can get. I had it. Congratulations to me.

But it didn't stop there; there was also one more gift I was given. And that was the gift of DID, Dissociative Identity Disorder (Multiple Personality Disorder) – well fuck me. I was later diagnosed with roughly around five different personalities. Now I know it sounds scary and it sounds really bad. But, you know, it is just a way that people survive. And it's a coping mechanism, that you adopt these different personalities to survive. It's a survival mechanism because what was happening inside my brain was that I was compartmentalising. I would come across a situation, and then I would lock it up, put it in a box and get rid of it and move on. And then I would find another problem, lock it up, put it in a box and move on. I had this storage container with all these boxes and all these different situations in them. Then every such time these different personalities would kick in and out to obviously protect me or serve whatever purpose to ensure that I was safe. If I didn't do this, I was told I would most likely be dead. And a lot of people have got these disorders and don't even know. But until you actually get diagnosed or actually start discovering or taking the steps to deal with these things, you won't fix them.

Crossroads

I remember I went back in one night to SA and got up to date with things in a circle. I remember it was my turn to talk and we had about three minutes to talk. I was recovering and I said the only reason was because I was also seeking help outside. Sometimes it's great to do a 12-step program because their steps are very similar to AA. Sometimes you've got to go outside and get professional help as well too. Most of these men just rely on this one thing, this circle of other men, and it's all well and good, but you've got to do other work to get there and fix yourself because every action has a reaction. If people smoke, and they smoke for a reason. If people drink, they drink for a reason. If people are angry and violent, they are angry and violent for a reason. If people go out and sexualise women, it's for a reason.

I mean, if you look back and you think about my story when I told you I was back in the army and the defence force, women were sexualised to me by these people that were in charge of me. They were my bosses. And then going back before that when I was a child growing up, my dad used to sexualise women in front of me. He did the same thing. I had no hope, but to come out on the other side. But the one thing that Ruth did say to me, is that I'd survived this long, so I was going to be amazing when I recovered. She said, "When you recover, you're going to be amazing, you're going to be better than normal. You're going to be above average because you've learned what it's like to be on that side of the fence. When you get to this side of the fence, you're going to have all this acquired knowledge and understanding to be able to help others." And that's exactly what I want to do to help other people, especially men. There are a lot of men out there and they need to just let go of the ego and just move forward and accept there's a problem that they need to fix. If they did that, the world would probably be a better place, especially when we're talking about people in power. And people who have a lot of money tend to be the worst obviously. It's everyone else's fault, right?

But yeah, this was an amazing discovery, a huge discovery. And when I came out of that first meeting with Ruth, I was so light, I was feeling absolutely wonderful about myself already. I couldn't believe how great I felt. I was drained and tired, but I was feeling great because finally, what I thought was going on inside of me was answered, it was finally written down on paper and it was answered. I was so blessed with this; to finally know. It took someone who is a professional that knows how to do a job to actually take me seriously and actually fix the problem, or at least help me fix the problem.

Chapter 10

REDEFINING MOMENTS

At this point, I started to pull back on a lot of stuff and started to realise exactly where I was situated in life. I was starting to actually see a lot clearer, seeing through the fog, and beginning to understand the benefits of having to fix myself. So, you know, one of the biggest things that I found in my journey in life so far is you've got to stop, and you've got to be present. No matter what you're doing in life, you've got to stop and be present. One of the things I also learned, even having children, is that you've still got to put yourself first. Because if you don't put yourself first, you're no good to anybody. You're absolutely no good to anyone, including your children. You do have to put yourself first, then come to the children, and then so on and so forth. But a lot of people think I'll put my kids first, or I'll put my wife first, or whatever it may be. No, you've always got to put yourself first. Because as I said, if you're not in the right mind, the right frame of mind, then your body's not going to work right?

The Wild Journey

I often use this as a way of explaining this to people; an analogy that your body is like a car. The outside of the car can look great, you can wash it daily, you can wash it once a week. You can spray this on it and make it smell nice, put this on it and wipe it and make it shine. You can add accessories to create and enhance features on the car and stuff like that. That's fantastic. But if you don't maintain the motor, that car will eventually stop working, no matter how great the surface looks. A lot of people like to have things looking great on the outside, and they like to tell stories and they like to build a persona that everything's great and fantastic. Social platforms such as social media are big for supporting these lies. But on the inside, the motor hasn't been changed and hasn't been serviced. This is exactly like what the brain needs, and if it's not serviced then it affects the body. The brain runs the body, there's no other way of saying it. So, if you're not right upstairs, the rest of your functionality, your body parts, are not going to work correctly.

So, I started to get myself and my brain in tune. And as I did, I started to realise that I needed a different career; I needed a different path in life. The next problem I had was that I really had no trade. I had no trade, no certificate to fall back on. I mean, what did security and being in the Army give me skills aside from to kill people? I mean, really, is that a certificate? Is that acceptable? Maybe you want to be a mercenary, or maybe you want to go back to the security industry, but not where I was now. I was wanting to go forward and keep going. It was one thing I always said to myself in life – I never want to go backward, and I don't intend to ever go backward. The day I go backward, then, obviously, I've got to rethink what I'm doing wrong.

I've always said I'll keep climbing that ladder, and I like to climb the ladder really quickly. Some people like to get to the top and

Redefining Moments

yell and scream out "Look at me, look at me". But eventually, the ladder is not stable, they haven't laid the foundations properly. And that ladder ends up falling. And that's one thing I've always said to myself, that if I'm ever going to start my own business or do anything like that, foundations need to be solid, they need to be rock solid. So, I kept going through and trying to work out what I could do.

One day it dawned on me. I was actually skilled in a couple of things. My partner at the time said, "Why don't you start a business doing magic?" Well, I laughed. I laughed, and I said, really? I mean, I'm going to make a career, I'm going to make a living out of doing magic tricks. Like people are going to pay me what $50 here and there to do a magic trick, really? So that went on the backburner. I did keep it in mind though, because I actually really was quite good at what I did, because I'd been doing it since I was six years of age. And so, this is where magic saved me – it actually did work.

I went for a job, an opening down at Dreamworld, one of Australia's largest theme parks and I went for it. It was entertainment, and I thought this was great. You know, this is who I am. This is what I need because I'm so artistic and so creative. I've never had the ability to do it because I've always been dulled down, always put into the dark because no one wanted to know about what I did, or could do. I decided I'm going to go for it. And I did, I went for it.

There were a whole heap of other people, and you know, look, I'll be honest, I was a bit intimidated because some of these people were very talented. There were dancers, singers, and sometimes there were people that could do all of that, you know, they could act too. There were triple threats. What could I do? I did some

The Wild Journey

drama back at school. And I could do magic. The thing was no one else could do magic like me. Then it dawned on me; I was original. I did all the tests, and I did all the character role plays and put on suits. They wanted me, and to see a trick. And I got the job. I was now a part of the Dreamworld team. I was a part of the entertainment department. And I stayed a part of that for two years.

It was fantastic because I became a resident magician out there. I had my own identity because what I didn't realise at the time was that I actually had something very unique that most of them if not all of them that were there didn't possess. I could actually do magic and act well. I was quite good at what I did, and I was quite skilled, so I started laying the foundations and I started using Dreamworld as a practicing ground. Then I did a Valentine's event in Brisbane, and I went out and started street busking. I was building up my reputation, but I was also building up my skill set as well. I had a feeling about what people out there liked and didn't like because I had no mentor when I grew up. There was no YouTube, there was no internet, there was nothing. It was the QBD bookstore and that was about it.

I became someone who was making people smile and joyful. I then thought to myself that I needed to keep doing this and create a skill set that people could see. And an opportunity came up in those two years, and I actually got to be the person who was on the same stage as a pre-show before the Wiggles came out. I was their support act before they came out. And there were like 4000 people jammed into this park at Dreamworld that day, it was huge. I still remember all these prams together; they were like cars in a carpark. A sea of prams lined up; it was amazing.

Redefining Moments

I then started building up my confidence, and I started working behind the scenes and building my business. And I thought I'll give this a go because I have a job here at the moment to support me. I have some sort of income, even if it was only casual. Because don't forget I was going through complex PTSD, and I wasn't well still and was in recovery mode.

One of the things that people don't understand when you've got Complex PTSD is that you burn out quickly. Normally if someone does an eight-hour day that's fine, but I get to about four hours, and I'm done. Your brain burns out because you're in such a heightened state of alert that you only go half the distance because you get tired out quickly. But people don't understand that. For me to achieve something as equal to someone who is an expert out there doing the same stuff is amazing because, I mean, I'm out there competing against people that don't have these issues holding them back or pulling them down. I'm competing with these people and I'm keeping up and then sometimes I'm actually doing better than them. And you know, it's very rewarding for me to know that.

There have been people in the industry of magic for millions of years – maybe not quite but for a long time. And I was doing leaps and bounds on top of these people, I was getting to meet celebrities, work with them on the radio, I was going on TV, I was really doing a lot of things to get my name out there and be someone fast. It was a catch-up game. And I started to realise that people paid really good money for entertainment, and really good money for magicians. And because I'd done stage illusions and I've done stage shows, I actually had the right to call myself an illusionist, because I actually was doing and performing illusions. It was another step up in the industry. And not all illusions need to be big and on stage either.

The Wild Journey

And so I became an illusionist. It's amazing because I started to get jobs, I started to get gigs, I started to get known through word of mouth, which is the ultimate thing in the entertainment industry. And I started to get all this work. I started off doing kids' stuff. And then I started building up my reputation and building websites, building up videos, and photos. I started to get really high-end VIP corporate gigs and to really get a name for myself as Drace illusionist, that was my stage, something we came up with. And it took off.

I was being respected and I was doing stuff that people were finding amusing yet intriguing. I was going to places where there were always happy times, someone's birthday or a wedding celebration, and so on. They were just like an hour, two hours, maybe three. And that's it. This was working out really well for me.

After two years Dreamworld had an incident where four people were killed on a ride, and I then had to obviously make that decision where to go. I was only casual, so because the park was closed and then restricted due to the incident, we started losing work. They started cutting back on staff in the park. They started playing around with rosters, and they started splitting shifts and making us work shit hours and days. So, I was starting to lose shifts because I wasn't going to go and start doing split shifts, you know, doing two hours or whatever in the morning then coming back doing another three or four in the afternoon.

I found that my gigs were starting to conflict with their rostered-on weekends and stuff, and I had to keep saying no, no, no. So eventually, I stopped going, and eventually, my contract was terminated because I didn't keep up attending. But having said that, they were already depleting the park by up to 70%

anyway. It was not just entertainers, but photographers, and people working food stands and rides. It was very disappointing because this could have been avoided. It was a human error. It wasn't something that just happened, it could have been avoided. Because of that, I eventually lost my position out there.

I then started working just on my gigs. And then I got to a point whilst I was working on these gigs, I was healing myself as well, so I was getting better and better and I started finding that these toxic people who had been in my life were just dissolving as my energy grew. And as I became more confident in myself, I found that this energy was creating new paths, it was creating new friendships and new work opportunities. When I started off it was just negative, I just sometimes still look back and I go you know that incident with Dreamworld with the four people dying, maybe it was a sign for me to move on, move out of there and start doing something different.

I kept at my business, and my business became hugely successful. Massively successful. And I've done so well, I've traveled, I've gone overseas and done some magic in New York and LA and also went to Alcatraz, in San Francisco, and done a straitjacket routine. My magic was flourishing. It was amazing. It was doing so well.

And then, unfortunately, a pandemic hit the planet.

The Wild Journey

Chapter 11

FEAR, ANXIETY & DEPRESSION

I want to take a moment to just establish exactly what was happening in my life at this point in time.

During the pandemic, I lost all my work as an entertainer. I decided to use the time to research and study, and I followed up on my lifelong dream of doing hypnosis. I now operate and own a successful business helping others in hypnotherapy and holistic work.

This ended up having a significant impact both on my life, and those of others.

The Wild Journey

I'd obviously decided to fix myself; to repair myself. I decided to take the time and effort, and use the resources available to me, to fix these things such as DID, Complex PTSD, depression, anxiety, memory loss, anxiousness, fear, phobia and fix it. And when I looked, one of the things that I naturally realised I was doing was being self-aware. When you become self-aware you start fixing yourself. When you cannot get off the lounge and you're waking up, breathing radically, finding your heart pounding and sweating, always over-analysing things, and overthinking things all the time – when you're doing these things, you're not living in the present moment. You're always thinking what if, you're always in that fight or flight mode, your amygdala activated. But the amygdala is actually a good thing, it helps us stay alive. It's an instinctive thing built in to ensure that we keep safe.

Unfortunately, what happens when you come across a traumatic situation is that the amygdala is activated, forcing you to choose between fight or flight, and you cannot turn it off sometimes. Or it reads everything wrong. You'll see this behavior in people when you know what you are looking for. Realising this, I can now see it a lot clearer, and I see people on the spectrum and understand their position. I'm able to identify these things just by reading their body language.

Throughout the course of my career one of the things that I have been professionally taught and have had to learn is body language. And it's instinctive to me now and it comes in really handy especially with the job that I do. In the two businesses that I operate, it becomes extremely important to be able to read other people's body language and understand exactly who I'm dealing with.

Fear, Anxiety & Depression

Did you know, most communication is physical? There's only a small percentage that is actually verbal. We're reading people's body language before we even talk to them. So, you know, a classic example is the arms crossed. I mean, most people know that doing that is closing yourself off; a person doing it will sometimes be on the defensive. But for me, I've come a long way, a long, long way.

People say, are you cured, are you fixed? I always go back to the analogy of the car. It might be running well, but you've got to keep it checked. And you've got to do that to yourself as well. You've constantly got to put yourself first. Always put yourself first. It's not arrogant. It's not ego. It's not selfishness. If I was ever going to give anyone any advice, it would be to put yourself foremost, first, okay? Because again, you're no good to anybody if you're not well, and I can't emphasise this enough. Especially those who are parents who have children, you need to be running 100%. You need to be fueled up mentally and physically and spiritually. You need to be 100%, because you've got a big day ahead of you and you've got children that look up to you and need your support.

So how did I overcome fear and anxiety? You know, when I was a kid, I was passing out and vomiting when I would give a lecture or stand up and speak. When I became the centre of attention, I freaked out. I would mumble my words. I was so anxious that my body literally shut down. There was a healthy dosage of being nervous.

As part of my other career as an entertainer, getting up on stage I'm always nervous because I'm always wondering, how is this going to play out? I've had many things go wrong over the course of my career. The best way you deal with these things is to laugh it off, honestly. Because something I learned in my industry as an illusionist, on the entertainment side of it, was that, you know, people were more critical, and people gave negative feedback to an entertainer and it still happens to this day, unfortunately, when they shut down, get upset and walk off. And that's it. So, you don't do that. The best thing you can do is to adapt to your environment and think what can I do from here? And sometimes, you know, you just have no second base to go to, so you just go hey, you know what, it's not working today. I'm out of magic, you know, and that's the line I used to use, I guess my magic ran out today. Of course, there are perfect magicians out there for whom nothing ever goes wrong – not.

So you know, it is what it is. But look in saying that, most of the strategies that I did use, and this isn't for everyone, but most of mine involved what is known as self-hypnosis. I didn't realise it. But now what I do as a master clinical hypnotherapist is that I realised going back that I actually was utilising this – I was naturally doing this. Because one of the things that I teach in my retreats now is breathing exercises. We do not breathe properly. We are shallow breathers. Breathing is key. It is absolutely key. Breathing is meant to be natural. It's meant to be easy. You're not meant to think about it. So, there are different forms of breathing out there. My breathing is very simplified but very effective and also allows you to be in the moment. A lot of people in this day and age are not present.

Counselor Deborah Brown said, just try an exercise. What I want you to do is to go there, and I want you to shut your eyes and count five things that you can hear, and five things you can smell. So, what you're doing is becoming present, you're becoming mindful. It's called mindfulness. And you're bringing yourself back and you're not overthinking, and it takes away the anxiety. It takes away the stress and it does work.

Fear, Anxiety & Depression

You know, there are exercises you can actually do when you're going to get triggered to prevent the trigger so that you keep from going into a rage. Because once you get to the rage, you can't pull back – at that point you're causing problems. You're causing destruction, you're causing hurt. You don't want to get there so there are techniques that I teach that will get you mindful of your triggers before you get to that point. And these are things I've learned myself. And what I teach people is all science-based. It's all social, socially accepted, it's socially proven, it's science, there is no trickery. There is no magic to this. It is the true essence of magic if you want to look at it like that.

So how I got over some of my fears, if not the majority of them, fears, phobias, anxiety, and all the rest of it, was to basically confront them. Now I do this a lot with hypnotherapy these days. I get people through hypnotherapy to do these exercises. But as I say, I somehow instinctively learned how to do these self-hypnotherapy exercises with myself. And so, for example, I always used to have dreams of falling. I had a fear of heights. I would stand up on something and if I looked down, I'd be terrified, absolutely terrified until my feet were back on the ground. It wasn't until I joined the army back in Townsville that I actually went in a plane and jumped out of it at 14,000 feet. I did it several times. I was scared, sweating, I was nervous, and I was unsure. But you know, at the end of the day it has to be done. I couldn't keep living like this. The idea of self-hypnosis was already playing out. I continue to do skydiving. Confronting fears, and direct exposure works for some, but not all – I must mention that. Everyone is different.

I also had a fear, a phobia, of sharks. I was terrified of sharks. And I mean the movie Jaws certainly didn't help as a young boy. I think, you know, most of us around that age when it came out

The Wild Journey

would remember that experience. I mean, to this day, there are a lot of people that reference Jaws as where their fear of sharks started. So, what did I do? I went scuba diving, and I went down the bottom and I saw sharks, and I realised that they're actually quite placid; they don't care about us. Of course, they'll be curious but they're actually not going to chase you. It was so beautiful to be down in that water with them. And I developed a different respect for the shark. You'll hear this a lot with people that do a lot of diving and do a lot of interaction down in the water, where there are sharks, and they say exactly the same thing. You just want to reach out and touch them. And I did want to reach out and pat one of the sharks, I never thought I'd say that.

I had a fear of being in small, tight, confined places, too – claustrophobia, which a lot of people do have. And so, what did I do? I went down to north New Zealand, and I went down into the caves, and I went down caving. And I went into small, confined areas that I could just fit through. These spots were also dark – there were spots where we turned off our torch lights, and our headlights, and we kept going through little waterfalls where there were pockets of water. We would stand up to our waist in confined spots, but I went there, and I loved it. It was just like a whole entirely different world down. It was so amazing. I was just fascinated.

The same with being on stage when I first did my magic show in front of people back at school. I mean it was a concert. I was so nervous, my presentation and my speech and everything were just all over the shop because I was just so nervous. I couldn't look people in the eyes. All I could do was look at the trick. Now I own the stage, I do presentations, and I now teach people in retreats. I'm now a leader because I've got people that want to be a part of my tribe and that want to learn from me because I've healed myself. And you can too, you've just got to follow the basic principles, and these are the three basic principles I'll give in this book right here right now.

Number one is to be mindful, be present. Be in the moment. Don't overthink and don't dwell on the past. Learn from the past but don't dwell on it. Be mindful when you're eating something, taste it, chew it. Be present. When you're talking to someone, make eye contact, look at them, and be present. Being mindful, and being in the moment is hugely important, and will stop a lot of anxiety and a lot of problems because what happens most commonly is we dramatise and catastrophise. This was something that I had initially with PTSD. Catastrophising is self-sabotage, don't do that. So be mindful, be present, and breathe.

Secondly, learn to breathe. Breathing is very, very important. As I said earlier, we are shallow breathers. We are not designed to be shallow breathers, but we do it. We need to understand that we should be breathing deeper. And when we breathe deeper, we breathe better. When we breathe better, our body functions better. Our brain functions better. Breathing is very important. If I can give you a tip in this book - right now, take three deep breaths in through your nose. Hold it for a few seconds and exhale out through your mouth. That's all you need to do. Three deep, mindful breaths all the way in, and hold it, and all the way out. Three, it's all you need.

The third one and the most important one is, as I said earlier, to always, always put yourself first. No matter what, put yourself first. If you're running well and you're okay and you're at 100% or close to it, then you can focus on the next person or the next situation. But always putting yourself first is vitally important. Always remember, if you're not running 100%, you're no good to anybody. You need to put yourself first, and that's without ego or being narcissistic. Unfortunately, some people out there don't know the difference.

And those are three tips that I'm giving you right here in this book right now. Okay, you need to understand those things.

My life is amazing right now. There are so many things happening, and there's so much to offer people; helping other people is an amazing thing. And if I could give you one more tip, just one more tip – go out and go do something nice for someone. It is the best dopamine you'll ever get. Trust me, go out and give someone a hug or buy them a coffee. A total stranger. You know, I'm not saying go and hug a stranger. I'm just saying go and buy a coffee for a stranger or do something that's really, really nice. You don't need to know who they are. They don't need to know what it's for. It's amazing. You've just made that person's day and you don't know how that person woke up. You don't understand if that person was on the verge of suicide. You probably saved a life. Always remember that. There's always something happening in someone's life, no matter how small or how big it may appear to you. But for them, it's everything.

Chapter 12

HEALED

As always, my story will continue to grow. And it hasn't stopped yet. It'll only stop the day that I'm buried six feet under. Until then I'll always have to keep maintaining myself, and I'll always have to keep doing check-ins. I'll always have to keep being accountable. I'll always have to keep learning about myself and learning about others, that's what this life is about. You only get to live this life once that we know of, I don't recall any other lives. I don't. But this is the one you're living in now. And the one thing that I would advise anybody if you've got an opportunity is that it's never too late to change things. It doesn't matter what your age or your circumstances are, it's never too late to change yourself to become a better version of yourself or the best version of yourself. You only have to take steps, one step at a time. You trudge the path if you need to. It may be hard; it may seem impossible. But it's not; it can be achieved, and you can achieve it.

The Wild Journey

One of the things I have followed in life is the hero's journey.

The hero's journey is a common narrative archetype, or story template, that involves a hero who goes on an adventure, learns a lesson, wins a victory with that newfound knowledge, and returns home transformed.

I believe in you because I now believe in me.

What I would like to say is that you need to put yourself first as I've explained previously, but for me, I'm in a place of really good opportunities and situations. For me now, I have come a long way. I'm so proud and I'll never go back to where I came from. I run two successful businesses, two entirely different businesses. I run an entertainment business called Smart Artz Entertainment, where I'm an illusionist, escapologist, mentalist, and comedy hypnotist and I go out and entertain people. That's what I do.

Then over on the other side, I'm a master clinical hypnotherapist and I heal and help people. And now I run retreats. At the moment I'm running half-day retreats and will eventually get into bigger retreats. And that's where my goal is and, you know, people have to have goals in life because that's the purpose of living right. You've got to set a goal no matter how small it is, no matter how big it is. It might be a goal to have a kid, it might be a goal to own a certain car, to marry a certain person. It doesn't matter what your goal is, but you always must have a goal, it's always nice to have a bucket list.

I've come a long way since the pandemic came into our life in 2019. Most people naturally lose a lot of work, especially in the entertainment industry. The government didn't want to do anything about incentives or do anything to try and build the entertainment industry back up here in Queensland. We still have poor restrictions in place which discriminate and segregate people who have been jabbed from those who have not been jabbed. You can't go into venues and events unless you get coerced into having jabs.

You've always got to have a secondary backup plan. You've always got to have something else up your sleeve. And this is something like a magician and no pun intended. I always had a sleeve. I always had an ace up my sleeve. And this is what you've got to do in life. You've always got to have that ace up your sleeve. I believe in it. You've always got to have a game plan A, plan B, even a C. But then what I have over here is I have a situation where I am now a clinical master hypnotherapist where I teach timeline therapy. I teach neurological and linguistic programming where I'm actually teaching people now how to hypnotise, how to be a clinical hypnotherapist.

I've met a beautiful partner now, her soul is amazing. Belinda has come into my life, and I believe for a reason. She understands me, she knows me, and she knows who I am. And she works with me. She doesn't work against me. She doesn't work around me. She works with me.

I've got a beautiful dog called Leon, who is an assistant dog, and he was assigned to me to help me with my PTSD, and Leon now is just a companion dog. He's just like anyone's dog that they have at home. He's food-focused. Absolutely. But, you know, he's amazing, and he's a big part of my life as well. Leon's taken me through some of those darkest moments, and he's been there. If I could suggest anything to anyone it's that pets are amazing, and if you go onto my website, www.acehypnotherapy.com.au,

The Wild Journey

you'll find blogs up there about how they set off your happy hormones, so it's worth a read.

I'm moving out to acreage very shortly, setting up a bigger retreat out there. I do my practices; I've helped so many people so far with so many different things and that's how I get my happy hormones. I said earlier, you know, going out and doing something for someone releases dopamine. That's how I get my dopamine, by helping people and seeing them walk in one person and walk out a completely different person, but for the better.

These are amazing times now; it's fantastic that I'm able to do this now. As my psychologist said, I still do check-ins and in fact, a lot of people don't realise a lot of psychiatrists and psychologists actually go to other psychologists and do check-ins because of the work they do. They get bombarded with a lot of negativity and a lot of information that they've got to keep to themselves, so they have to obviously have to air that out somehow. I still keep in touch with mine every so often and remain accountable.

Being accountable is hugely important. It doesn't mean you are silly; it doesn't mean that you don't know what you're doing. That you can't control yourself. It's just being accountable. It's making sure that your engine is running well. It's that checkup I'm talking about – you do have a car, right? So that's exactly what I do.

I'm now no longer on medication. Psychiatrists are nothing but legalised drug dealers in my opinion. They'll just push out pills. And a lot of the problems I see today are that it's easy for people to just get prescribed something and jump on it and have tablets. And look, don't get me wrong, there's a time and a place for medication, for all sorts of medication down to those that fix headaches. But that doesn't resolve the problem. It doesn't fix the problem. That's why I do a thing called timeline therapy because I go back, and I go back to the root cause of these problems like fear, anger, anxiety, depression, all that because it's still there. Believe it or not, if you jump off those tablets, it'll still be there. Whilst you're on the tablets, the idea is to fix the problems and go through and understand the problems. But the problem is you feel so good when you're on them you think the problems are gone. You think it's not there anymore, and you're better. But then when you come off them and you slowly decrease the dosage, you start to realise you're not. It's still there. I've been in that situation, and then I realised, whoa, hang on a second. Stop. I need to go back on them and work on this and fix this.

I've done timeline therapy with another hypnotherapist, and I dealt with some of my issues, and they worked, absolutely worked. Again, it's all based on science, and science is real. I just wanted to say that what we do in life, and how we perceive things is totally up to us. We are in control, and for those who don't know, hypnosis is self-hypnosis; no one can put you in a trance, only you can put yourself in a trance. This is why I now teach self-hypnosis at my retreats because people have a better understanding of how it works, and how to do it and the results and the effects are amazing. I just want to leave that there and just let you know that in life, there are always going to be challenging situations.

If someone gets out there as a life coach or whoever they may be and says they found the cure; that they now no longer have issues in their life. You know, they're financially set, they've got everything sorted. It's likely in most cases all baloney because these people still have situations in their life. And I know certain people that have said this and gone on social media platforms and said how amazing they are now they found God, they found the truth, they found how to work this out, they're debt-free. I'll say you've got to do your homework. You don't go out there and buy the first car, you go out there and have a look around. There are so many cowboys and cowgirls out there ripping people off. Whatever you choose to do out there, always remember to put yourself first, be the best version of yourself, and make sure that you live life because you only get to live it once.

This is something that was written on a card and given to me that I keep to this day, this reminds me and puts me back in the scope of my path.

Everything happens for a reason. And even though the reason is sometimes unclear, I graciously accept that it unfolds through love, in accordance with the divine will of my soul.

ABOUT THE AUTHOR

Drew Glebow is currently a certified Master Clinical Hypnotherapist and a qualified coach and trainer in Neuro-Linguistic Programming (NLP) & Timeline Regression, work which he undertakes both nationally and internationally. Drew also specialises in Erotic Hypno, helping endless amounts of individuals and couples find true pleasure within themselves and their partners. On top of this, Drew is a Reiki practitioner, card reader, sound healer, and breathwork – as well as ice/cold exposure – instructor.

If that wasn't enough, Drew is also one of South-East Queensland's most sought-after and diverse entertainers in Australia, going under the stage name of Drace. Drew has five decades of experience in magic, and over ten years of excellent five-star service as an owner-operator of Smart Artz Entertainment. He has always employed professional entertainment to all. Drew is one of two Sensory Illusionists in the world, with an arsenal of skills in close-up, parlor and stage illusions, comedy hypnosis, mentalism, and escapology.

Drew first discovered his love of magic at six. By the time he was 13 years old, he had been on national TV performing magic. By 14, he was performing as a child at children's birthday parties for payment. He later worked at one of Australia's largest theme parks in Queensland, Australia, as a resident magician before heading over to the United States of America where he further entertained at the Magic Castle and escaped from a strait jacket at Alcatraz Island in San Francisco.

Over the years, Drew has entertained millions of people, from television to live performances. There has never been a job too big or too small or an audience he has not been able to wow, from family children's birthday parties to adult VIP corporate events.

Drew also believes in delivering entertainment that brings wonder, and that if you open up to that wonder, you allow joy in your life. Joy brings happiness, and a lifetime of memories of your special day. This is the true magic.

We may biologically get older, but the inner child lives on in us all.

OFFERINGS

As a Master Clinical Practitioner in Hypnotherapy, Neuro-Linguistic Programming (NLP) and Time Line Regression, I am able to offer my services and training to both those wanting to become therapists, or those who just want to add to an already work-life skill set. As a qualified coach and trainer, I am able to run courses and certify those who wish to advance their skills or their own self or loved ones. I also hold retreats for individuals, families, or groups, be it clubs or workplaces.

Please visit my website for full details at www.acehypnotherapy.com.au

ACKNOWLEDGMENT

I would like to make mention of the fact that if I had not reached out and contacted Ultimate 48 Hour Author, this book would not have been written yet, if at all. This book has become a lifelong dream to write, continuing my knowledge and skills long after I have gone.

I would also like to give thanks to Jo, my previous partner of six years, for coming into my life when you did, and rather than putting me down and insulting me, taking my potential good qualities and helping me rise back to the top of the ocean. Unfortunately, the relationship diminished due to the drain that had on you by being the rescuer. I have no idea where I was heading before you but I felt it was going to be tragic.

I'd also like to thank my mother Lynn for all you have done for me over the years. For the reassurance and protection you offered in those times of need, as any mother would. You lied at times to save my ass or help me press forward. You know what those moments were.

Acknowledgment

To my two beautiful daughters, Charlie and Kelsey. You are what keeps me honest and helps me to break the traditions of generational trauma, allowing you to be free of suffering and pain and have a chance in life to create a beautiful family home for your children and grandkids.

Finally to my current partner Belinda. Thank you for being the understanding and kind person that you are and for the skills you have to see that I am continuing to make those correct choices. Even though we may disagree on some, we agree to disagree and move forward with the intentions of working more on ourselves.

For living is the intention of learning and loving.

www.ingramcontent.com/pod-product-compliance
Lightning Source LLC
Chambersburg PA
CBHW041308110526
44590CB00028B/4292